DISCARD

OLIVER GOLDSMITH

She Stoops to Conquer

EDITED BY

VINCENT F. HOPPER and
GERALD B. LAHEY

New York University

WITH A NOTE ON THE STAGING

GEORGE L. HERSEY

Bucknell University

ILLUSTRATIONS BY

FRITZ KREDEL

BARRON'S EDUCATIONAL SERIES

Great Neck, New York

THEATRE CLASSICS FOR THE MODERN READER

To reproduce the values and effects of the theatre on the printed page is the ambitious aim of this series of the classics of the stage. Although good plays have always been read as well as acted, few playwrights before the era of Ibsen and Shaw have ever written with any public other than the theatre audience sharply in their minds. In consequence, the reader of older plays is usually required to supply his own visualizing of the staging and his own interpretation of stage action and even the manner of the delivery of the lines themselves. Frequently he is also required to put up with abbreviations and other space-saving printing devices.

This modern reader's edition of theatre classics vitalizes the outstanding plays of the past with the kind of eye-pleasing text and the kinds of reading and acting guides to which today's reader is accustomed in good published editions of twentieth century dramas. The text itself has not been altered except for occasional modernizations of spelling and punctuation (common to all modern editions of earlier works) and the rare use of italics for emphasis when the reading of a line is not immediately clear. Essentially, that is, the author's text is as he wrote it. Added to it are descriptions of scenes and costumes, indications of expression and action, and explanation of words and references not readily comprehensible.

The illustrations should aid immeasurably in visualizing the play. A description of the original staging, stage conditions, and stage techniques is provided partly as still another aid to visualization but principally to show how the playwright adapted his materials to suit the particular stage conventions of his time. Companioning each play are also a sketch of the author's life, an analysis of the play, and a selective bibliography to make this as much an all-in-one edition as possible.

She Stoops to Conquer

THE PLAYWRIGHT

Of the many writers of comedy who were blown by the winds of chance or fortune eastward from Ireland to London—Goldsmith, Congreve, Sheridan, Wilde, Shaw —Goldsmith has been the most sentimentally treated by history. Unlike Wilde, who has been attainted with an odour of depravity, Goldsmith is generally pictured as the happy, innocent, wayward child of genius, as far removed as possible from the "ambiguous" artist of Thomas Mann. Especially picturesque are the accounts of him as the vagrant flutist and ballad-maker, singing and charming peasantry and villagers into providing him with food and lodging as he makes his way on foot through Flanders, France, Germany, Switzerland, and Italy—a trip later to be commemorated by his poem *The Traveller,* praised by Johnson as the best verse since Pope. Frolicsome and merry, tip-full of practical jokes and hearty Lumpkin gaiety, Goldsmith is the antithesis of the sophisticated Congreve, man of fashion and elegance.

Even in his darker days when he first descended upon London as a hack-writer and denizen of Grub Street, his living from hand to garret, his intervals of fevered feasting alternating with enforced fasting are treated as "picturesque," a part of the loveable and laughable story of Goldy. He is a prototype of the figures in *La Vie de Boheme*. No sketch of Goldsmith is complete which does not picture him reduced to one blanket (a sort of woolen stocks with two holes pierced through it for the arms of the hapless author) calmly enduring the harrying of a scolding, demanding landlord. And then his rescue by Johnson or some other protector, and a quick return on borrowed money to Madeira, beef, truffles, etc. This is the irresponsible light-hearted Goldsmith of the garret before it became a Latin Quarter "studio."

Goldsmith's literary productions were slight but varied. He attempted many forms of composition, always with success: the essay as in *The Citizen of the World;* the sentimental novel, *The Vicar of Wakefield;* verse as in *The Traveller* and *The Deserted Village;* comedy, *The Good Natured Man* and *She Stoops to Conquer.* All are marked by his grace, ease, naturalness.

As for his choice of a career, Goldsmith's vocational contemplations were as varied as his types of composition. He successively considered teaching, the Church, the Law, and then medicine; apparently he did actually take some sort of degree in Leyden, though his practice seems to have been limited to a few prescriptions rejected by apothecaries as works of fancy rather than of therapy. As for his literary vocation, he is as unlike the austerely and arrogantly dedicated Stephen Dedalus as possible; Goldsmith backed into his trade while retreating from other vocations, embracing it as the last refuge of a hungry man.

Some of the facts of his life are as follows: he was born in November, 1728, in Ireland, the son of an impoverished Protestant clergyman; he moved in his very early years from the county of Longford to the hamlet of Lissoy, county of Westmeath. Lissoy is perhaps commemorated as Auburn in his *Deserted Village,* an eighteenth century *Grapes of Wrath,* conceived in a mood of pathos and nostalgia:

> . . . desolation saddens all thy green:
> One only master grasps the whole domain,
>
>   .   .   .   .
>
> And trembling, shrinking from the spoiler's hand
> Far, far away thy children leave the land.
>
>   .   .   .   .

Ill fares the land to hastening ills a prey,
Where wealth accumulates, and men decay:

. . . . .

But a bold peasantry, their country's pride,
When once destroyed, can never be supplied.

. . . . .

. . . . trade's unfeeling train
Usurp the land, and dispossess the swain;

Perhaps the principal event of Goldsmith's early life in Ireland was a savage attack of small-pox which left him pitifully marked for life. As he was small, awkward and ungainly, this additional affliction helped further to make him a chopping block for the local wits, rustic and often brutal. His early reticence and shyness won for him the characterization: a "stupid, heavy blockhead." All of his life, Goldsmith suffered from a desperate lack of self-confidence, especially among people of eminence or fashion, although he could be robustly, prankishly happy in the tippling, ballad-singing company of tavern jokers. This curious split in his nature is projected in the character of Young Marlow, who is so stammeringly and awkwardly ill at ease with Kate Hardcastle but so sprightly and happy in the presence of tavern companions. Another aspect of this timidity, this intense shyness, was that on occasion—if opportunity permitted—Goldsmith gave himself absurd airs. This tendency manifested itself in him early: at sixteen, released from school, a guinea burning in his pocket, he stopped overnight in a small village on his way home, where he was directed to the house of a local squire as an inn. Goldsmith assumed the grand manner, even to inviting landlord, wife, and daughter to a bottle in the supper-room; the story has it that the landlord played along amusedly so that Goldsmith had the mistakes of an evening available for his later comedy. We see this aspect of his character when the nervously shy Marlow parades himself before the supposed bar-maid as a dazzling London rake. At times a bit of success drove Goldsmith into London society foppishly attired with sword, gold-headed cane, blue silken breeches, fancy wig, etc. Doubtless the more natural side of his character is commemorated in the gaiety of Tony Lumpkin and The Three Pigeons, the latter being reminiscent of Conway's Inn of Goldsmith's post-college days in Ireland.

Boswell's references in his life of Johnson to Goldsmith's ineptness in conversation underlines this unhappy social timidity. Johnson remarked of him: "Goldsmith should not be forever attempting to shine in conversation; he has not the temper for it, he is so much mortified when he fails . . ." We recall Marlow's anguished mortification at his failure in the interlude with Kate Hardcastle. Writing for the periodical *The Bee* in 1759 in a vein of personal whimsy and self-confession, Goldsmith said: "For my part, . . . I was never distinguished for address, and have often blundered in making my bow, . . ." Naturally Goldsmith was delighted at Johnson's account of the latter's unexpected meeting with the King in the Royal Library. After hearing Johnson's account of the episode, Goldsmith complimented him, saying that he had done ". . . better than I should have done; for I should have bowed and stammered through the whole of it." Perhaps the interview between Kate and Marlow is a fancied projection of this kind of situation, so harrowing to the shy Goldsmith.

Nor was his shyness helped by his situation at Trinity College, Dublin, whither he went after his village schooling. Goldsmith's sister having become engaged to a rich man's son, the father made it a point of honor to provide her with a substantial dowry. In doing so he exhausted the family fortunes. The result was that Goldsmith had to attend Trinity as a sizar, that is, as one who gets free lodging and the scraps of the commons kitchen; in return for this, he does menial chores. He must also wear a distinctive garb to indicate his inferior status. At first Goldsmith refused to attend Trinity on such terms; but his kindly Uncle Contarine persuaded him to do so. What is not clear is why this same generous uncle did not supply him with enough money to lift him above the embarrassment. Only a few years later, we find him generously supplying Goldsmith with pounds and pence. At any rate, it was as a sizar that Goldsmith attended Trinity. In the college-entrance examination list, Goldsmith was at the bottom; when he took his degree in 1749, he was also at the bottom of the list, one of the few pieces of consistency in his life.

Returning home after taking his degree, Goldsmith spent a desultory existence, finding his few moments of idle happiness at the near-by tavern. Finally, reminded that he should be up and doing, he elected at length to become a physician. He spent some time in Edinburgh studying—presumably—and more time at Leyden, being in the latter city for about two years. Very little in detail is known of his racketing about Europe, as records and letters have been lost or destroyed. At any rate, his continental junketings provided the materials for *The Traveller,* a poem of later date. Eventually he returned to London (February of 1756) without resources and faced with the need of daily bread. In London during these years, Goldsmith was for a time an usher at Dr. Milner's Peckham School; then meeting a bookseller through the Milners, he worked as a literary hack; small successes alternated with more solid failures and garret solitude.

He worked at odd literary jobs, such as that of compiling and making digests of long works so that they would be available in capsule form for those with limited time for literary indulgence. Both Goldsmith and his biographers have pointed to this moment as that in which the patron had disappeared and a large buying public not yet arrived. Goldsmith inveighs heartily against the situation, protesting that the writer is now the tool of the book-seller and must express not his own personal vision of life but provide only those wares commercially useful to the bookseller.

If one examines Goldsmith's literary work at this period, one is struck with the fact that thus early in his career Goldsmith had developed his stylistic trick of a rather formal balance and antithesis, a device of style as evident in his prose as in the verse of Pope. It is notable that even when he later writes dramatic dialogue, most of the characters (as in *She Stoops to Conquer*) speak in this manner. There is a parallelism of syntax: that is, adjective-noun construction for adjective-noun, prepositional phrase balanced against phrase, etc., but with an opposition of meaning. Almost too frequent to warrant notice, a few instances may be set down:

MARLOW: In good inns　　you pay dearly for luxuries
　　　　 In bad inns　　 you are fleeced and starved

———

MISS NEVILLE: The disorder of your dress
　　　　　　　　　　　　　　　　will but show
　　　　 The ardour of your impatience

———

HASTINGS: I'm surprised that one who is
　　　　　　　　so warm a friend
　　　　　　　　　　　　　　 can be
　　　　　　　　so cool a lover

———

So that　　　with eating above stairs
　　　　　　　　　　　　　　and
　　　　　　drinking below
　　　　　　　　　　　　　　with
　　　　　　receiving your friends within
　　　　　　amusing them without, etc., etc.

———

If you find their reason manageable, you attack it with your philosophy

If you find they have no reason, you attack
them with this

———

OLD HARDCASTLE: This may be
                modern modesty
      But I never saw anything look so like
          old-fashioned impudence

———

MISS HARDCASTLE: But I vow   I'm disposing of the
              husband
                     before
        I've secured the lover

———

In this hypocritical age, there are few
    that do not
          condemn in public
          what they practice in private

———

I hope, Sir, a conversation
          begun with a compliment to
          my good sense
          won't end with a sneer at my
          understanding?

Then at times the point-for-point antithesis assumes a
duet form:

MISS HARDCASTLE: He met me with a respectful bow, a
          stammering voice, and a look fixed
          upon the ground

OLD HARDCASTLE: He met me with a loud voice, a lordly
          air, and a familiarity that etc.

If one compares this style with Sheridan's, for example,
it will be clear how much the antithetical mannerism had
grown upon Goldsmith much as the paradoxical epigram
falls from the lips of all of Wilde's characters.

One of the productions of Goldsmith's hack-writing
period was entitled: *Enquiry into the Present State of*

Polite Learning in Europe, published in April of 1759. Among other things, he attacks critics as natural enemies of artists. Goldsmith remarked that a critic need follow only two rules: 1) observe that the work under review could have been much improved by more pains, 2) fulsomely praise some one else. He presents a cyclical view of culture in which decay inevitably ends with the critic: "Ancient learning may be distinguished into three periods: its commencement or the age of poets; its maturity, or the age of philosophers; and its decline, or the age of critics." In his more direct attack on the critics, Goldsmith presents them as being pretty much what Congreve presented in his critical fop Petulant in *The Way of the World:* "Though ill-nature is far from being wit, yet it is generally laughed at as such. The critic enjoys the triumph, and ascribes to his parts what is only due to his effrontery."

In our own day, when there is so much rather conventional and jargon-laden complaint about the commercial dilution of culture owing to the "mass market," "mass media," and "mass culture," it is interesting to observe Goldsmith's objection to his moment of history, the patron having vanished: "The author, unpatronized by the great, has naturally recourse to the bookseller . . . It is the interest of the one to allow as little for writing, and for the other to write as much as possible: accordingly, tedious compilations and periodical magazines are the result of their joint endeavors. In these circumstances the author bids adieu to fame; writes for bread; and for that only imagination is seldom called in." The passage no doubt recalls Goldsmith's struggles of the years preceding its writing.

However, the publication of the *Enquiry* marks the beginning of a period of greater success for Goldsmith. In the year following, he contributed his "Chinese Letters" to Newbury's *Public Ledger* and met Dr. Johnson. In 1762, his letters were published as *The Citizen of the World;* purporting to be the observations of a Chinese on European culture, they are obviously the reflections of a European on those aspects of his own culture least gratifying to him. In 1762, Goldsmith also published the life of Richard Nash, the Bath Beau and master of ceremonies at the fashionable watering place. In 1764, *The Traveller* appeared, and Goldsmith was made a member of the famous Literary Club. Goldsmith was fortunate to have won the interest of Dr. Johnson, who early recognized his talents and praised and befriended him. For all of Goldsmith's charm and graceful vivacity as a writer, he must have seemed a pigmy among such giants as Gibbon, Burke, and Johnson. In 1766 his *Vicar of Wakefield* was published; the manuscript of it had been earlier sold by Johnson for sixty pounds, which Johnson had duly conveyed to the garret-bound Goldsmith for his release from bondage. In 1768, Goldsmith had his first play produced: *The Good Natured Man;* in 1770 *The Deserted Village* appeared; and in 1773 *She Stoops to Conquer* successfully attacked the sentimental tradition of the comic stage.

Within a year of this success, Goldsmith was dead. Despite his run of successes, he continued to be in financial difficulties; with declining health, he could no longer bear his poverty lightly, and as his temper became increasingly irritable, he passed into ever deeper moods of despondency, then of despair. He died miserable and apparently without his many celebrated friends being really aware of his great distress. Although Sheridan was to die in similar misery after a more brilliant career, the titled and the famous followed his body to its rest in Westminster Abbey. When Goldsmith was buried privately in Temple Church ground in April of 1774, it does not appear that Garrick, Johnson, Burke, Reynolds, or any of his friends paid him this last respect. Goldsmith was himself a brilliant composer of epitaphs; if Johnson's commemorative words were not brilliant they had the more appropriate virtue of sincerity: "Let not his frailties be remembered; he was a very great man."

THE PLAY

Any comment on the play *She Stoops to Conquer* must begin with pointing out that Goldsmith, along with Sheridan, decried the tradition of the "sentimental" comedy, the *comédie larmoyant* in which tears flowed and laughter languished—to parody Dr. Johnson's declaration concerning the serious drama of the eighteenth century in which "declamation roared while passion slept." Sentimental comedy, inspired by the Muse of the Woeful Countenance was a new form of comedy, its starting point being a reaction against the comedy of Etherege, Dryden, Wycherly, and Congreve, the New Comedy aiming at a purer, a more edifying, a more didactic form. Since sentimental comedy was born of a reaction against Restoration Comedy, the latter must be considered briefly.

At first glance, the Restoration period, the last four decades of the seventeenth century, seems separated from us by the chasm of time, of things silently gone out of mind—especially in its manners and costume. The literary and social expression of the interval 1665-1700 is the sunset period in the autumnal gardens of Courtly Society, that society in which, as Charles Lamb said, pleasure was duty and the manners perfect freedom. The King, his courtiers, and their friends constituted a small, homogeneous group who gave the tone to the manners and theatre of the time.

But viewed from within, the Restoration age, with its carefully knotted silken cravats and satin waistcoats, is not so far distant. In its philosophical outlook, it is no further away than the rebellious, agitated, iconoclastic, defiant decade of the Twenties. The young men of both periods were a Lost Generation, the Restoration young men being more "gay" than "sad." But there were both types in both periods. The nocturnal spectacle of Sir Thomas Ogle, Wilmot, the young earl of Rochester (in some ways a titled prototype of Scott-Fitzgerald), and the earl of Dorset brawlingly drunk on the tavern balcony at Oxford Kate's of London, haranguing a motley multitude in the street below and irreverently laughing at everything except bottle and boudoir, is not so far removed from the flippancies and orgies of the expatriates of the Twenties in Paris and along the Riviera, and in the speak-easy belt at home.

Both the young generation of the Restoration and that of the Twenties came to maturity in the wake of a devastating, costly, and brutal human struggle; both looked back on the past with a sense of spiritual malaise, with a sense of repudiation. For although rips and revellers were of the long-suffering and eventually triumphant Cavalier party in sympathy, they had, like our own writers of the Twenties, the disposition to utter their malediction on both houses. Both generations in repudiating the past and moving out of an old order of values and belief passed into a kind of psychic vacuum. They were spiritually isolated and left to find their values for themselves through their own feelings and imaginations and contacts with life. As the Twenties repudiated in orgiastic fashion the manners and values of Victorian gentility, so did the Restoration generation violently repudiate the constraints and confinements of Puritanism and at the same time quietly sterilize the moral influence of the religious tradition of Cavalier Anglicanism. War and chaos had been the tutors of the period of Hemingway, Edna Millay, T. S. Eliot, Ezra Pound, Scott-Fitzgerald. The same tutors had been busy with the Restoration gallants.

We might consider very briefly just one play of the period, one that is by no means the hardest expression of the period, such as Wycherly's *Country Wife,* or Eth-

erege's *Man of Mode* might be considered. Congreve's
Love for Love is one of the more mildly amusing of the
Restoration comedies, less outspoken and frank in its
dialogue, less disturbing in its characterization. It was
Congreve's concession to "popular" drama and his most
liked comedy. Yet even that, good-natured for a Restoration play, scarcely offers the spiritually minded any con-
solation. The two principal lovers in the comedy are
brothers: Ben, the sea-going man, and Valentine, the
sophisticated townsman. When Ben sings of rivalry in
love, we are transported to something like a Las Vegas
night-club:

> The soldier swore like thunder
> He loved her more than plunder;
>
> .   .   .   .
>
> The tailor thought to please her
> With offering her his measure.
> The tinker too with mettle
> Said he could mend her kettle
> And stop up every leak.
> But while these three were prating,
> The sailor slily waiting,
>
> .   .   .   .
>
> And then he let fly at her
> A shot 'twixt wind and water,
>   That won this fair maid's heart.

Granted that sea-going Ben needed a little "polishing,"
as his father continually affirms, his fashionable, courtly
brother Valentine in love with the fine Angelica speaks
of another ravishing lady as follows:

"Pretty round heaving breasts, a Barbary shape, and a
jut with her bum would stir an Anchorite, and the prettiest foot! Oh, if a man could but fasten his eyes to her
feet, as they steal in and out, and play bo-peep under her
petticoats!" There is little more of elevation in the civil-
ized townsman.

When the whimsical ingenue Prue is being taught the art of courtship and being initiated into the sacred rites of love by Tattle, the fop, the dialogue is as follows:

TATTLE: And won't you show me, pretty miss, where your bed-chamber is?

PRUE: No, indeed, won't I; but I'll run there and hide myself from you behind the curtains.

TATTLE: I'll follow you.

PRUE: Ah, but I'll hold the door with both hands, and be angry;—and you shall push me down before you come in.

TATTLE: No, I'll come in first, and push you down afterwards.

PRUE: Will you? then I'll be more angry, and more complying, . . .

Restoration comedy, this Utopian citadel of self-indulgent moral egotism, of cheating wayward wives and double-dealing friends, of chilling *sang-froid* and cynical sex-intrigue, of predatory gallantry and passionless passion, of finicking fops and cuckolding courtiers, was eventually laid siege to and conquered. Throughout the Restoration period, the ladies in the boxes protested against the theatre's violation of taste and propriety, and their opposition and protests finally bore fruit. The official opening assault on Restoration Comedy, not so much causing the change of mood as giving expression to it, was Jeremy Collier's *Short View of the Immorality and Profaneness of the English Stage* . . . published in 1698. It was a "short view" in every sense; especially in its implied philosophy of what comic drama should be. However fanatical and narrow Collier may have been, historians concede he had "cause" for his perturbations and certainly tongue for their utterance. But the change had already been anticipated and had been, like a tidal wave, under way for some time. Not only had "the ladies" maintained their opposition, but even arch-offenders like Dryden had admitted in stray passages to the debasement of literature and the stage. Colley Cibber in his *Love's*

Last Shift had in the middle of the last decade of the century anticipated the new comedy eventually to be called sentimental comedy. A contemporary critic Davies had noted the advent of this new comedy by mentioning its greater purity of manners, its decency of language, the unexpected reconcilement of erring characters, the remorse and the penitence, the rapturous pleasure of the audience expressed in the shedding of honest tears of happiness.

If Collier was the parson who officiated over the burial of the old and the baptism of the new comedy, Colley Cibber and Richard Steele were the midwives who assisted at the birth of the new comedy. By the end of the first quarter of the new century (1725), sentimental comedy, the reaction to Restoration *ethos,* was fully established and perhaps the dominant form. Steele had written in a mood of unhappy reflection ". . . the accomplished gentleman upon the English stage, is the person that is familiar with other men's wives, and indifferent to his own; as the fine woman is generally a composition of sprightliness and falsehoods . . ." Steele finally recorded his hour of triumph in writing an epilogue for a play of Shakespeare: he vehemently castigates one of the principals of those Restoration stage gallants, Dorimant of Etherege's *Man of Mode:*

> The perjur'd Dorimant the beaux admire;
> Gay perjur'd Dorimant the belles desire:
> With fellow-feeling, and well conscious gust,
> Each sex applauds inexorable lust.
>
> .   .   .   .
>
> Love, glory, friendship languishing must stand,
> While sense and appetite have sole command.

The adjective term in sentimental comedy is the source of some vagueness: not only is the term variable in meaning as used by different people, but its relation to "sentiment" and "sentiments" (often meaning *views, attitudes*) and "sententious" further clouds it.

In *The Way of the World,* Mirabell, the leading character, has been speaking reproachfully to Millamant, the heroine; he concludes: "I say that a man may as soon make a friend by his wit, or a fortune by his honesty, as win a woman with plain-dealing and sincerity." To this the beautiful Millamant answers: "Sententious Mirabell!" Obviously this term has nothing here to do with facile, over-responsive feelings, or false, shallow feeling. It refers simply to Mirabell's rather satiric habit of aphorism, of disparaging summing up of human nature. He is not in any sense a "man of sentiment," however, as the phrase is applied to Joseph Surface in *The School for Scandal.*

In *Lady Windermere's Fan,* a comedy of the 1890's by Oscar Wilde, there is a conversation in the chambers of Lord Darlington, in which the latter defines a cynic as "a man who knows the price of everything, and the value of nothing." To this his interrogator replies: "And a sentimentalist . . . is a man who sees an absurd value in everything and doesn't know the market price of any single thing." Obviously the former refers to a coldly intellectual and narrowly amoral appraisal of life, whereas the latter considers the sentimentalist as one so overcome or so victimized by facile emotion as to have distorted and unreal values. Obviously too a sentimentalist need not be a "man of sentiment," for the man of sentiment, Joseph Surface, utters lofty inanities and moralizing commonplaces which he neither feels nor means; and the sentimentalist, on the other hand, may be quite inarticulate.

The psychologist William James illustrated the character of the sentimentalist when he told of the rich lady who sat in the comfortable, warm theatre weeping copious tears as snow in the form of paper confetti drifted across the warm stage to fall on the studious arranged rags of the forsaken, homeless maiden (a highly paid actress) while the weeping spectator's coachman, half-frozen by the zero weather, sat outside waiting for her. Sentimentalism is here something unreal, a false response to a small part of a total situation, and hence a distortion of reality.

Let us look at the "man of sentiment" as the phrase is used in dramatic tradition. In *She Stoops to Conquer,* Miss Hardcastle says to Young Marlow, during the course of their first interview: "Indeed I have often been surprised how a man of sentiment could ever admire those light airy pleasures, where nothing reaches the heart."

She speaks, mockingly of course, and the key word is "the heart"; it implies a moral seriousness and heavy earnestness of attitude. And as Young Marlow stumbles out of her presence in confusion and haste, she laughingly observes:

"Was there ever such a sober sentimental interview?" "Sober" because "sentimental"; the words exclude light-hearted merriment and frivolous laughter. The reference to "man of sentiment" (it appears repeatedly in Sheridan's *School for Scandal*) is to a person, who, sincerely or insincerely, is devoted to the utterance of lofty inanities, of feeble-thoughted, high-minded cliches, of shallow, idealistic dullness. Of course the "sentiments" and the "man of sentiment" may be quite false: in *The School for Scandal,* Joseph Surface is the Restoration cynic turned into hypocritcal man of sentiment, unctuously sermonizing in public and cynically frank only in soliloquy:

All in all then, the term "sentimental" suggests something false, facile, unreal; and "sentiment," tedious moralizing, a kind of affected, artificial seriousness, repressive of buoyancy of spirit, gaiety, laughter.

The new or sentimental comedy as it developed placed great emphasis on a plot which presented virtue suffering yet triumphant, of heroes and heroines who tirelessly utter the banal didacticisms referred to just now as "sentiments." There is an abundance of "conversions" usually brought about as the final curtain falls upon the play, with orgies of repentance, of generous reconcilements as the erring and the wayward are reclaimed to righteous living by the spectacle of the virtuous, and the sinning are reprieved on promise of reform. Matrimony becomes not only respectable but purifying and stabilizing:

"Long toss'd in youth, that stormy time of life;
Our safest port is a kind virtuous wife."

Furthermore, poetic justice is observed in sentimental comedies with an almost fierce literalness. Anguished virtue is always rewarded at the end with a rather suspect promptitude and abundance; heroes and heroines who appeared to be making magnanimous and noble sacrifices under the impulsion of fine feelings have after all been inadvertently investing their virtue at 10% in a rising market. For at the fall of the curtain, it appears that the sacrifice was verbal only. Such a morality is after all suspiciously materialistic since we are urged to be good because "virtue pays." Likewise the villains are all punished suitably or generously forgiven on promise of reform amidst voluptuous swellings of the repentant and reconciled heart. As for virtue itself, its career in sentimental comedy made it increasingly boring, yet increasingly successful in attaining material reward: the honorable or priggish young man inevitably gets girl *and cash*. What makes such comedy false and unreal is that although we like to see the good and the noble and the deserving richly rewarded, we all know that in real life it seldom works out so patly. A comic vision which presents the reverse of this fact is necessarily "sentimental."

Sentimental comedy was produced to satisfy the taste that William Dean Howells imputed to his contemporaries when he declared that their ideal literature was a tragedy with a happy ending. Voltaire humorously re-

ferred to the new comedy as "tradesman's tragedy," referring in part to the more miscellaneous middle-class
audience of the Restoration. Finally, sentimental comedy
produced a conscious, theoretical *raison d'etre*: comedy
should not supply merely negative guidance to life by
realistically ridiculing and exposing the vicious and the
foolish; it should positively inculcate an ideal; the theatre
should wear a steeple on its head and church-bells on its
ears and present positive figures of virtue, goodness, be-
nevolence; it should supply a pattern of conduct, be
normative and didactic.

Not that the old comedy had not been moral; but it
had been moral in a different sense. It supplied real information about real life; it said "This is the way things
are; beware!" It was not comforting; its realism was a
flower with a thorn attached. Farquhar for example de-
fended Congreve's *Old Bachelor* on moral grounds, in
that it inculcated worldly wisdom. He pointed out that
the play's moral was that if an old man marries a young
wife, he need not show surprise that she is unfaithful to
him. In Farquhar's own idiom: "Fondlewife and his
young spouse are no more than the eagle and cockle; he
wanted teeth to break the shell himself, so somebody else
run away with the meat—here are the precepts, admoni-
tions and salutary innuendoes for the ordering of our lives
and conversations couch'd in the allegories and allu-
sions." But this kind of comedy was marked by raillery,
vigorous satire, ruthless intellectual ridicule. It wielded a
cold, clinical dissecting knife.

The embroidered handkerchief succeeded it. In the
new comedy the head was not worn on the shoulders; the
heart was worn upon the sleeve. The triumph of sentimental over Restoration comedy was a triumph of morals
over manners, of "sentiments" over witticisms, of insi-
pidity over satire, of simpering over cynicism, of blarney
over irony, of sermonizing over sophistication, of self-
righteous sensibility over worldly sense, of remorse, re-

pentance, and conversion over wine, women, and the way of the world.

The question then about such comedies as those of Goldsmith and Sheridan is—to what extent do they recover the spirit of the Restoration, the old comedy; to what extent are they still a part of the tradition of sentimental comedy, the tradition which they were attacking?

Before attempting an answer to this historical question, we note the fairly conventional outer structure of the play: there are the two young couples balanced against the old couple. The tavern prankster, Tony Lumpkin, is also present but he acts not only as the comic spectacle of the unlettered rustic but as the controlling force of the plot, for it is Tony who not only creates the basic situation of mistaken identity on which the play turns so persistently (and which is elaborated by Kate Hardcastle) but who also purloins the ill-fated cask of jewels and superintends the absurd night-journey to Aunt Pedigree's Crackskull Common. He is more important, for example, than is the rustic booby, Bob Acres, of Sheridan's *The Rivals,* both as a character and a plot architect. When Tony can't read, we laugh at him; but when he so joyously provokes Old Mrs. Hardcastle's fury about the stolen jewels, we laugh with him. He is both tavern buffoon and country joker.

As for the old couple, so common to eighteenth century comedy, their ludicrous traits of character are in almost the same antithetical balance as is Goldsmith's prose. Just as Mrs. Malaprop is absurd in her miscarried pretensions to learning, so is Old Mrs. Hardcastle absurd in her pretensions to being a woman of fashion. The pretension provides an amusing scene in which the fashionable Hastings ironically compliments her on her raggletaggle elegance. In contrast to Mrs. Hardcastle, who professes to be abreast of the times, is Mr. Hardcastle, whose antiquarian crochet is to be in perpetual remembrance of things past, thus rendering his rambling, old-fashioned house mistakable for an inn, and himself an eccentric innkeeper.

As for the two young couples, there is both contrast and similarity in their situations. Hastings is in contrast to Marlow, the former a poised and self-possessed man of worldly fashion, quite equal to all social situations, the latter, tormented by shyness and stammering insecurity when in company of ladies of high fashion, but aggressively confident with women of low station. Since Old Mrs. Hardcastle favors the marriage of Miss Neville to Tony, Hastings and she have a barrier to surmount, elopement without jewels is not quite satisfactory. Since Marlow is so abashed and retreating in her company, Kate Hardcastle has to resort to the role of the pursuing woman to corral her quarry.

The comedy turns partly on the growingly apoplectic indignation of Mr. Hardcastle at his treatment at the hands of his guests; like old King Lear little by little his indignation expands until the containing walls of patience and forbearance give way—and the situation becomes clear (at last) to Young Marlow—or almost clear. And in part, the comedy turns on the successive roles played by Kate: first, that of the brisk, comely barmaid, then that of the poor but virtuous cousin. Marlow's varying response to her real personality and to those impersonations give rise to confusion in the mind of Mr. Hardcastle (and through him, of Sir Charles Marlow) as to Marlow's true character as a ladies' man.

She Stoops to Conquer is certainly not a return of the Restoration drama; neither is it particularly reminiscent of the ensuing sentimental comedies. Rather it is an agreeable blending of farce, satiric comedy of manners, and sentimental comedy. In its theme of mistaken identity it is basically farcical. Goldsmith's uncertainty about his title indicates some confusion in his own mind as to whether he was writing an uproarious farce or a comedy of manners. It was advertised by what is now its secondary title: *The Mistakes of a Night,* and he once thought of calling it *The Old House a New Inn.* Seeing in Kate Hardcastle a new type of heroine, an unsentimental young lady of great charms, who could resort to disguises and deceptions to get her man, who could in the guise of a barmaid parry deftly the advances of the gay gallant without loss of lady-like dignity, Goldsmith finally gave the play its present title. Reynolds wanted to call it (after Farquhar's *The Beaux's Stratagem,* which it mentions and to which it has basic resemblances) *The Belle's Stratagem.* Goldsmith apparently agreed that the intention of the play was to present a new type of anti-sentimental heroine, quite free of simpering and suffering virtue and quite briskly managerial, but he shied away from a too direct comparison with Farquhar. The present title was borrowed doubtless from his admired Dryden, who had written:

"But kneels to conquer, and but stoops to rise."

Viewed from the standpoint of comedy of manners, the satiric spirit, the ridicule, the larking and laughter of Restoration comedy are there, but the coarseness of language, situation, and character-type has been extinguished. It is Restoration comedy "converted" and baptized. There are no fops, no cuckolds, no sex-intrigue of a cynical sort, or even seriously irregular young men. Marlow's interest in ladies below stairs seems rather perfunctory; he is more of college sophomore on the town than a kitchen-maid's Casanova. In respect to the Restoration duel-of-the-sexes (not to be confused with the psychologically morbid battle-of-the-sexes of Strindberg, Lawrence, O'Neill) there is little trace. In the old comedy, the love-duel (the love-duet of Romeo-Juliet reversed), a contest of wit and urbanity between male and female, proceeded from an equality of the sexes socially and was based on an assumption of a fair degree of heart-wholeness and heart-freeness on the part of both. The love-duel presupposed that marriage was a surrender of cherished individuality and independence not easy to part with, together with a lurking feeling that the compulsion of the marriage bond would prove irksome and withering, that monopoly threatened spontaneity. At the same time there was also a true, strong sex-attraction: hence the attempt on the part of the superficially haughty, cool-tempered hero and heroine to preserve within the domestic fold as much privacy and personal freedom as possible.

This resolution took the form in the old comedy of "proviso" scenes, in which each party, half-mocking and half-serious, listed in itemized form the conditions and "terms" on which one would consent to be "enlarged" into a husband and "dwindle" into a wife. Such scenes are presented in Dryden's *Secret Love,* Etherege's *Man of Mode,* Sedley's *Bellamira,* and culminate in the verbal duel between Millamant and Mirabell in *The Way of the World.* Hence even with one's foot on the first tread of the stairway to marriage, such proviso scenes were the vehicle of wit, ridicule, amusement. In the sentimental tradition the solemn couple approached marriage heavily, *au serieux.* Laughter was not one of the sacraments, not even a part of the rubrics. Richard Steele, for example, reproved the love-game approach to marriage on the grounds that it involved insincerity and frivolity; at such moments Steele wished to emphasize the more tamely decorous and un-Wilde-like importance of being earnest. In this regard, *She Stoops to Conquer* is closer to the canon of Steele than to that of Congreve. To be sure Kate Hardcastle's adoption of trickery and amiable deception was thought a little unladylike by contemporaries, slightly compromising to true virgin dignity. Yet the situation was forced upon her owing to Marlow's peculiarities; she did not voluntarily embark upon her escapades as a natural expression of her temperament.

From our vantage-point she is merely the jollifying, mischievous inverter of convention, the light-hearted improvisor of method, but serious as to her ultimate goal. Basically, as she and Marlow join hands and hearts at the end, there is the true "union of souls" demanded by the sentimental tradition, yet not without overtones of the fun and amusement lingering from the chase. And there is still another bit of shading we should not forget. When Kate's father describes Marlow before his arrival, she is quite frankly attracted by good looks and not overly concerned about the condition of his soul, an attitude which is emphasized by having the father comment upon it. Such an attitude is lacking in the "ennobling" quality sought for by the sentimental tradition. Goldsmith had delicately blended the two traditions.

Again something of the realism of the old comedy is present in the tavern scenes of The Three Pigeons where fun is openly made of gentility and the latter's aversion to low scenes of real life, because not edifying. Hence the tavern frequenters mockingly protest their hatred of all that is "low."

Although the play is enveloped in a zany, zestful, hearty fun-and-games atmosphere comparable to that Victorian medicine-ball of fun, *Charley's Aunt,* this character of "healthy" laughter can hardly be labeled as sentimental. Except possibly for one point: there are no villains in the play; everyone is basically good-natured and well-meaning. There are follies but no vices; at the end, all is reconcilement and forgiveness for the mistakes of an evening.

If the character of Kate is cleanly and antiseptically non-sentimental, that of Marlow is more ambiguous. There is just a touch of the sentimental prig about Marlow when he is being cross-examined by Hastings concerning his intentions toward the "tempting, brisk, lively little thing," etc. At first glance, he appears to be the cynic who knows the market-price only, for he says, "I don't intend to rob her . . . there's nothing in the house I shan't honestly pay for." But on further questioning,

when Hastings speaks of Kate's virtue (on Hastings' part
the scene is ironical, he knows what Marlow does not
about Kate), Marlow suddenly becomes "fine":

"And if she has, I should be the last man in the world
that would attempt to ruin it."

The implication of the scene is that Marlow thinks that
most barmaids are already debauched; if not, he nobly
refrains. He appears to be somewhat improbably a fash-
ionably-dressed buyer whose eccentric point of honor
permits him to purchase only damaged goods at reason-
able rates. Obviously the passage is intended to draw a
line between Goldsmith's hero and the Restoration rake
and profligate who like many passengers on ocean liners
delight not only in first serving but (with courtesy of the
management) at no charge. And not even eighteenth
century bar-maids wore small labels announcing whether
or no. It is this uncertain element that suggests the
namby-pamby, shilly-shally element of sentimental
drama: Marlow is a trifle naughty, but protected by a
severe statute of limitations.

More significantly, Marlow in his last encounter with
Kate as the poor cousin has one foot on land and one
in water. It is the sentimental scene in which virtue, impoverished and forlorn, conquers pride of caste and
affluence, the melting heart overwhelming the muddled
head:

MARLOW: (*aside*) "This girl every moment improves
upon me. (*to her*) It must not be, madam. I have already
trifled too long with my heart. My very pride begins to
submit to my passion. The disparity of education and
fortune, the anger of a parent, and the contempt of my
equals, begin to lose their weight . . ."

MISS HARDCASTLE: "Then go, sir . . . I must have only
the memory of your addresses, while all your serious aims
are fixed on fortune."

MARLOW: "By heavens, madam, . . . Your beauty at
first . . . But every moment steals in some new grace

. . . What at first seemed rustic plainness, now appears
refined simplicity. What seemed forward assurance, now
strikes me as the result of courageous innocence and
conscious virtue."

That is the true sentimental note; not merely "beauty"
but "courageous innocence and *conscious* virtue." Following upon the fulsomely antithetical style of address,
Marlow flings himself upon his knees—and then all is
capped with that most dubious device of the sentimental
writer. For all of Marlow's noble willingness to sacrifice
fortune, paternal approval, education, respect for friends
to the imperious influence of maidenly innocence and
"conscious" virtue, the old dodge of the sentimental
comedy bobs up again. No real sacrifice has been made;
fortuitous reward follows verbal profession which need
never be really tested. For Kate is after all the daughter
of landed gentry, of the comfortably "fixed" and highly
respectable Mr. Hardcastle, and with an education and
social style somewhat superior to that of the kneeling
hero. The noble revolutions of the heart turn upon a sham
axle.

Still, even here, we must make some qualifications; for
at the height of this orgy of high-mindedness, of the
pseudo-rake suddenly turning honorable, sacrificing
suitor, the tender, moist, fruity joy which should clothe
the soul of the spectator (like the donning of slightly
damp, cold linen for a dinner-party) is interdicted. For
all during the scene Kate is light-heartedly mocking and
debonairly parodying her own role of virtuous heroine
with oglings and ironic overtones to the audience. Like
Miss Neville she makes a counterpoise to the sentimental
gesturings of her suitor;—we recall that on the verge
of elopement Hastings, in a declamatory mood, is willing
to abandon Constance's jewels and grandiosely perorates:
"Perish fortune! Love and content will increase what we
possess beyond a monarch's revenue . . ." Upon which
inflamed sentiment, Miss Neville sprinkles cool sense:

"In a moment of passion fortune may be despised, but it ever produces a lasting repentance."

Here a good conscience is quite frankly related to cash in hand. And in this kind of contrast of his male and female sensibility, Goldsmith has delightfully blended the solemn, serious *comedie larmoyant* with the sprightly, spirited laughing comedy of fun and ridicule, the latter prevailing over the former.

Certainly to many of Goldsmith's contemporaries, the play did not appear funny side up. Coleman, for example, the manager of Covent Garden Theatre, was especially fearful for the effect of Mr. Hardcastle's gathering of uncouth servants, Diggory et al., upon the refined wits and beaux of the period. Horace Walpole, a refined and somewhat precious observer of the day (who was not above referring to Goldsmith as that "inspired idiot"), has recorded after witnessing the play that Goldsmith ". . . has written a comedy—no, it is the lowest of all farces; it is not the subject that I condemn, though very vulgar, but the execution. The drift tends to no moral, no edification of any kind—the situations . . . make one laugh in spite of the grossness of the dialogue, the forced witticisms . . . the characters are low, and aim at low humour . . ."

Clearly Walpole gazed at the play through the pearl and gold lorgnettes of the sentimental viewer: the pursuing woman with her stratagem of deception was of course "vulgar;" it certainly was not "genteel" with its servant-buffoons and Pigeon-gentry; and there was no sermonette. With all the ludicrous misunderstandings and the good-natured spoofing of the sentimental hero— there was no ideal pattern of behavior presented. Walpole's criticism clearly reveals the sentimental formula of evaluation and not that of Dr. Johnson who declared that the end of all comedy was to be entertaining. And Johnson was entertained.

THE STAGING

Physically, the eighteenth century theatre was very much like that of our own day; it was, in fact the beginning of the modern theatre. The Renaissance and baroque drama of the preceding sixteenth and seventeenth centuries had possessed two quite different traditions. First, there were the popular plays presented commercially in theatres often improvised from inn-yards and indoor tennis courts. Here, as far as production was concerned, the rule of economy prevailed and there was a minimum of scenery. The audience, standing in the "pit" or seated in the encircling galleries, surrounded the actors, who performed mainly on an apron platform that projected well out from the stage proper. But if the physical characteristics of the popular theatre were meager, the intellectual and psychological ones were not. The intricacy of Renaissance plots is famous, as is the richness and variety of metaphor in the actors' lines.

The second tradition which developed during the years preceding the eighteenth century was that of the court gala, especially gotten up to celebrate the marriage or coronation of some member of the ruling family. Here, elaborate scenery and costumes were primary attractions, and no expense was spared. Fantastic palaces, at the wink of an eye, were changed into gushing fountains, rocky eyries, or distant battlefields. The actors in these masques (as they were called) were sometimes professional, but often members of the court; even kings and queens took part. Needless to say, no great histrionic demands were made upon the participants. Indeed, in a masque, the plot was perhaps the least significant consideration.

In the eighteenth century these two traditions united into one which still persists today. From the popular theatres of Shakespeare and Molière came the notion of a highly plotted narrative demanding considerable acting ability; and from the court masque came the tradition of quickly changing painted scenery.

In England, with the eventual relaxation of the 1737 law which governed the licensing of public performances, the popular theatre could operate more freely. Theatre-going became a fashionable recreation, and producers in the so-called "illegitimate" houses were able to realize a profit even in their smaller auditoriums. In London there were buildings such as the Opera House in Haymarket boasting enormous stages which could accommodate the full machinery for descending clouds and rushing rivers — effects still called for in Italian operas. But most eighteenth century theatres were more modest in their dimensions; often their stages were tiny by modern standards. Sometimes there was barely room for the actors.

Whether the stage was large or small, the scenic equipment was something like this. On either side of the stage was a set of wooden frames, which could run on and off stage in grooves in the floor, suspended overhead on a wheel and track system such as we sometimes see used for sliding barn doors. These wooden frames were covered with canvas and hid the offstage portions of the theatre. They were called "wings." Much larger frames, called "flats," operated in the same way but met in the center to provide the back wall of the set. Across the top of each set of wings was a canvas strip called a "border" which extended across the stage and served as masking to hide the upper part of the stage house from the audience. All these scenic elements were painted to represent some indoor or outdoor scene.

When the locale of the play had to be changed, the wings and flats could be drawn offstage in their grooves, revealing another set of flats and wings with a different scene painted on them. All details of a given scene were painted on the flats, even furniture and properties, except for those objects which the actors actually used. Eighteenth century actors rarely sat down so there was not apt to be much furniture about.

The stage opening, or proscenium arch, was often elaborately decorated, and usually boxes for the spectators were housed in it. From these box seats you could easily look down on the apron, but you could not see the stage proper without craning your neck. This indicates that the apron was where the actors spent most of their time, the area behind being reserved mainly for scenery. Thus the eighteenth century stage-setting was more of a *backing*

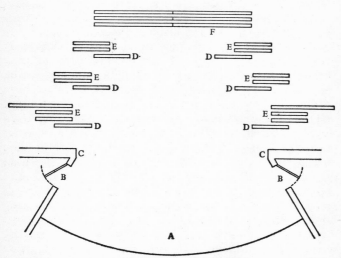

Diagram of a typical late eighteenth-century stage

A is the apron upon which most of the action took place; B, the proscenium doors; C, the proscenium opening behind which the curtain hung. The onstage wings are marked D, and those off-stage, awaiting their turn to be used, are marked E. Behind the first set of wings are a pair of shutters which can close the stage completely off for scenes in hallways and other constricted quarters. The back shutters are marked F.

for the actor, in contrast to the modern set, which *encloses* him. On each side of the proscenium arch was a door which led from the offstage area to the apron. Actors made their entrances and exits through these doors or through the spaces between the wings.

The audience not only occupied the normal orchestra seats, but also several tiers of boxes which curved around the inside of the auditorium like giant horse-shoes with their open ends toward the stage. Many of the older theatres in this country, such as the Metropolitan Opera House in New York (1882) still retain this horse-shoe arrangement for box seats and balconies. This form may have had its origin in the converted inn-yards where popular theatre was staged in the sixteenth and seventeenth centuries.

This picture of a typical eighteenth century theatre, as we remarked at the beginning, reminds us of a modern theatre, especially compared to what had gone before. But if our theatres have changed only a little and if we still occasionally use wing and border sets, there are important differences between our method of staging a play and the traditional method of the eighteenth century. One of these differences involves a whole new attitude towards change of scenery. In the eighteenth century theatre, the curtain was not closed at the end of a scene. Instead, a uniformed factotum came out after the actors had left and removed or rearranged all the properties for the next scene. Then the wings and shutters slid back, and the borders were raised *a vista* (in sight of the audience) by unseen hands backstage, revealing the new set in the manner described above. These *a vista* changes were part of the fun of going to the theatre, and audiences might well have felt cheated if the curtain had hidden them. As a matter of fact, this popular relic of baroque theatre practice did not disappear until the last century.

While the modern theatre-goer, schooled in the complete representationalism of Hollywood and Broadway, may object that these painted scenes must rarely have been very convincing, let him remember that the revealing brilliance of modern electric lighting did not yet exist. Eighteenth century scenery was lighted only by the flickering of myriads of candles. Chandeliers were hung backstage between the wings and borders, and also out in the auditorium. These auditorium lights, by the way, were *not* extinguished during performances.

Another important difference between eighteenth century practice and our own lies in the sphere of costume. In the eighteenth century no distinction was made between "modern dress" and "period" productions. An actor, whether he played Hamlet or an eighteenth century gentleman, wore either everyday dress or a kind of special "actor's costume" such as we see in Watteau's paintings of Italian comedians. One actress of the period, it is recorded, did give a Roman matron the classic toga she deserved, but insisted on wearing it over a hoopskirt!

This everyday eighteenth century dress was quite elaborate, however. Men wore black or white silk stockings and pumps decorated with fancy buckles. Their trousers consisted of tight breeches buckled just below the knee. They also wore capacious waistcoats and jackets with skirts or tails in back which descended to the knees. Lace bands were worn at the neck and lace cuffs at the wrists. The three-cornered hat with cockade or feather and the inevitable white-powdered tie-wig topped off the ensemble. The men of the eighteenth century had no compunctions about wearing bright and highly decorated materials, brocaded or printed in strong and colorful patterns. The tradition of black, brown, and gray which now dominates men's everyday dress did not set in until the nineteenth century.

Women wore pumps, too, and long stiff skirts and bodices as colorful as the men's suits. Skirts were almost always worn over hoops, and were often split up the center to reveal a contrasting underskirt. Sometimes panniers (wicker or wire frames which expanded the apparent width of the hips) were worn instead of hoopskirts. Over these the skirts were often draped in festoons which could end in short trains. Women's bodices were cut to a sharp point at the waist and in a very low curved or square neckline. Sleeves were elbow length, terminating in lace ruffles. White powdered wigs, very high, were

worn by all fashionable women for dress occasions, often
in combination with plumes.

The elegant everyday dress, the *a vista* scene change
(which probably groaned and creaked enormously), the
lighted auditorium, and above all the artificial quality of
the painted wings and flats — these things are to be kept
in mind when we try to reconstruct the production of
eighteenth century plays. Remember, too, that the play
was not a classic when it first appeared. Audiences did
not listen in worshipful silence. Perhaps they found themselves more amusing than the play: at any rate they were
apt to chatter during many of the scenes, and only during
the most important speeches by favorite actors and ac-
tresses was there absolute silence. During these scenes the
fans punctuated every particularly good line with salvos
of applause. At the end of the play the manager would
come out on the apron and if he was greeted with hisses
and boos he would retire in defeat, knowing that the play
was a failure and that it could not be repeated. If, on the
other hand, the audience's reception was reasonably en-
thusiastic, he would announce triumphantly: "The unpar-
alleled success of the latest and brightest spark from the
anvil of the comic muse will be repeated every evening
until further notice."

For the eighteenth century audience, the theatre was
more than a playhouse; it was a place where invitations
were issued, assignations made, duels arranged, debu-
tantes introduced, dowries settled, and reputations made
and lost. It was a glittering spectacle of fashionable dress
and histrionic partisanship.

DEDICATION

TO SAMUEL JOHNSON, LL.D.

Dear Sir,

By inscribing this slight performance to you, I do not mean so much to compliment you as myself. It may do me some honor to inform the public, that I have lived many years in intimacy with you. It may serve the interests of mankind also to inform them, that the greatest wit may be found in a character, without impairing the most unaffected piety.

I have, particularly, reason to thank you for your partiality to this performance. The undertaking a comedy, not merely sentimental, was very dangerous; and Mr. Colman, who saw this piece in its various stages, always thought it so. However, I ventured to trust it to the public; and though it was necessarily delayed till late in the season, I have every reason to be grateful.

I am, dear sir,
Your most sincere friend,
And admirer,
OLIVER GOLDSMITH

CAST OF CHARACTERS

in the order of their appearance

HARDCASTLE, an old-fashioned country squire.

MRS. HARDCASTLE, his fashion-loving wife.

MISS HARDCASTLE, their pretty daughter.

TONY LUMPKIN, Mrs. Hardcastle's son by a previous marriage.

HARDCASTLE

MISS HARDCASTLE

MRS. HARDCASTLE

DIGGORY, the Hardcastle's farm hand.

SIR CHARLES MARLOW, a member of the London gentry.

YOUNG MARLOW, his diffident son.

HASTINGS, close friend of Young Marlow.

MISS NEVILLE, Mrs. Hardcastle's niece.

MAID in the Hardcastle household.

LANDLORD in the nearby country inn.

also SERVANTS and DRINKING COMPANIONS of Tony Lumpkin.

SIR CHARLES MARLOW

YOUNG MARLOW

TONY LUMPKIN

SYNOPSIS OF SCENES

The entire action takes place in a small English village, about a day's carriage distance from London.

ACT I

SCENE ONE. A living room in the Hardcastle mansion, late afternoon.

SCENE TWO. The taproom of The Three Pigeons, shortly thereafter.

ACT II

The Hardcastle living room, a few minutes later.

ACT III

The same; about three hours have elapsed.

ACT IV

The same, an hour later.

ACT V

SCENE ONE. The same, some two hours later.

SCENE TWO. The back of the Hardcastle garden, shortly thereafter.

SCENE THREE. The living room, immediately following.

PROLOGUE

BY DAVID GARRICK, ESQ.

(Enter Mr. Woodward,[1] dressed in black, and holding a handkerchief to his eyes.)

Excuse me, sirs, I pray—I can't yet speak—
I'm crying now—and have been all the week!
" 'Tis not alone this mourning suit," good masters;
"I've that within"[2]—for which there are no plasters!
Pray would you know the reason why I'm crying?
The Comic Muse, long sick, is now a-dying![3]
And if she goes, my tears will never stop;
For, as a player, I can't squeeze out one drop;
I am undone, that's all—shall lose my bread—
I'd rather, but that's nothing—lose my head.
When the sweet maid is laid upon the bier,
Shuter[4] and I shall be chief mourners here.
To her a mawkish drab of spurious breed,
Who deals in *sentimentals*, will succeed!
Poor Ned[4] and I are dead to all intents;
We can as soon speak Greek as *sentiments!*[5]
Both nervous grown, to keep our spirits up,
We now and then take down a hearty cup.

---

[1] A popular comic actor.
[2] A parody of Hamlet's dejected speech to his mother, Act I, Scene 2.
[3] Referring to sentimental comedy of tears and virtue in distress.
[4] Edward (Ned) Shuter who acted the part of Mr. Hardcastle.
[5] Inflated, artificial moral rhetoric that aims to be edifying.

47

What shall we do?—if Comedy forsake us!
They'll turn us out, and no one else will take us.
But why can't I be moral?—Let me try:
My heart thus pressing—fix'd my face and eye—
With a sententious look,[6] that nothing means
(Faces are blocks in sentimental scenes),
Thus I begin—"All is not gold that glitters,
Pleasure seems sweet, but proves a glass of bitters.
When ignorance enters, folly is at hand;
Learning is better far than house and land.
Let not your virtue trip; who trips may stumble,
And virtue is not virtue, if she tumble."
     I give it up—morals won't do for me;
To make you laugh, I must play tragedy.
One hope remains,—hearing the maid[7] was ill,
A *doctor*[8] comes this night to show his skill.
To cheer her heart, and give your muscles motion,
He in *five draughts* prepared, presents a potion:
A kind of magic charm—for be assured,
If you will swallow it, the maid is cured:
But desperate the Doctor, and her case is,
If you reject the dose, and make wry faces!
This truth he boasts, will boast it while he lives,
No poisonous drugs are mixed in what he gives.
Should he succeed, you'll give him his degree;
If not, within he will receive no fee!
The college *you,* must his pretensions back,
Pronounce him *regular,* or dub him *quack.*

---

[6] Solemn and pompous.

[7] The muse of satiric, laughing comedy.

[8] The author, Dr. Goldsmith.

ACT ONE

Scene One

A living room in the large rambling old-fashioned country mansion of the Hardcastles. It is one of the many rooms that served no particular function in homes of the days when economy in building was of little importance. The rear wall is dominated by a large fireplace and is otherwise decorated with a set of the famous Hogarth prints depicting the "Rake's Progress," a pictorial representation of the downfall of a young wastrel. A screen stands toward the back near the left wings. Nearer the front at the left is a heavy round mahogany table, bearing a silver service with cups and saucers, with two or three chairs with brocaded backs and seats placed near it. A large comfortable armchair and another occasional chair are at the right, near the fireplace. The stage wings to right and left lead to other rooms on the ground floor. The proscenium door to the right leads through a corridor to other rooms and eventually to the outside front door; the left hand door opens into a hall and a staircase to the second floor. Nothing in the room is new, but everything is of the best quality, slightly worn but suggesting the ancestral wealth and station of the line of country squires who have been its successive owners.

In the late afternoon of this presumably spring day, its present owners, Mr. and Mrs. Hardcastle enter the room from the right engaged in a typical family argument. Mr. Hardcastle is a rather short and distinctly rotund country

49

gentleman in his fifties. A solid conservative, he lives in the glorious past when Prince Eugene of Savoie and the Duke of Marlborough led England and her allies to victory over Louis XIV in the War of the Spanish Succession (1701-13). From flaxen wig to knee breeches, his clothing is somber and conservative. Mrs. Hardcastle, a stout woman only slightly younger, finds her second husband difficult to get along with. She yearns for the latest fashions and London Society, but yearns in vain. Her husband's fixed ideas restrain her dress and confine her to rural circles. She wears her own hair which protrudes loosely around the edges of her lace-frilled cap, and her brocaded loose-fitting jacket and very full skirt are only moderately colorful.

MRS. HARDCASTLE: (*in a tone of mingled distress and habitual chiding*) I vow, Mr. Hardcastle, you're very particular. Is there a creature in the whole country, but ourselves that does not take a trip to town now and then, to rub off the rust a little? There's the two Miss Hoggs, and our neighbor, Mr. Grigsby, go to take a month's polishing every winter.

HARDCASTLE: (*in heavy complacent sermonizing accents*) Ay, and bring back vanity and affectation to last them the whole year. (*with extreme scorn*) I wonder why London cannot keep its own fools at home. In *my* time, the follies of the town crept *slowly* among us, but *now* they travel faster than a stagecoach. (*brightening with self-satisfaction as a brilliantly corrosive epigram comes to his mind*) Its fopperies come down, not only as inside passengers, but in the very basket.[1]

MRS. HARDCASTLE: (*bridling, and seemingly oblivious to her husband's witticism*) Ay, *your* times were fine times, indeed; you have been telling us of *them* for many

---

[1] A suggestion of extreme superfluity, since the basket of a stagecoach, attached to the back, was intended for luggage but sometimes was used for excess passengers.

a long year. (*calling attention to the old-fashioned character of the room with her hand*) Here we live in an old rumbling mansion, that looks for all the world like an inn, but that we never see company. (*with increasing exasperation*) Our best visitors are old Mrs. Oddfish, the curate's wife, and little Cripplegate, the lame dancing master; and all our entertainment your old stories of Prince Eugene and the Duke of Marlborough. I *hate* such old-fashioned trumpery.

HARDCASTLE: (*ignoring her absurd and frivolous fancies*) And I love it. (*mellowly*) I love everything that's old: old friends, old times, old manners, old books, old wine; and, I believe, (*ogling her fatuously*) Dorothy, (*taking her hand and patting it*) you'll own I have been pretty fond of an old wife.

MRS. HARDCASTLE: (*pulling her hand away sharply*) Lord, Mr. Hardcastle, you're forever at your Dorothys and your old wifes. (*with spirit*) You may be a Darby, but I'll be no Joan,[2] I promise you. I'm not so old as you'd make me by more than *one* good year. (*challengingly*) Add twenty to twenty, and make money of that.

HARDCASTLE: (*with pretended concentration*) Let me see; twenty added to twenty—makes just fifty and seven.

MRS. HARDCASTLE: (*flaring up*) It's false, Mr. Hardcastle; I was but twenty when I was brought to bed of Tony, that I had by Mr. Lumpkin, my first husband; and he's not come to years of discretion yet.

HARDCASTLE: (*quickly*) Nor ever will, I dare answer for him. (*with heavy sarcasm*) Ay, you have taught *him* finely!

MRS. HARDCASTLE: (*dotingly*) No matter, Tony Lumpkin has a good fortune. My son is not to live by his learning. I don't think a boy wants much learning to spend fifteen hundred a year.

---

[2] "A Darby and Joan" was a common expression to describe an old contented couple.

HARDCASTLE: (*exploding*) Learning, quotha![3] a mere composition of tricks and mischief!

MRS. HARDCASTLE: (*to whom Tony is perfect*) Humor, my dear; nothing but humor. Come, Mr. Hardcastle, you must allow the boy a little humor.

HARDCASTLE: (*with outraged vehemence*) I'd sooner allow him a horsepond. If burning the footmen's shoes, frighting the maids, and worrying the kittens, be humor, he has it. It was but yesterday he fastened my wig to the back of my chair, and when I went to make a bow, I popped my bald head in Mrs. Frizzle's face.

MRS. HARDCASTLE: (*with plaintive resignation*) Am I to blame? The poor boy was always too sickly to do any good. A school would be his death. (*optimistically*) When he comes to be a little stronger, who knows what a year or two's Latin may do for him?

HARDCASTLE: (*scoffingly*) Latin for *him!* A cat and fiddle! No, no, the alehouse and the stable are the only schools *he'll* ever go to.

MRS. HARDCASTLE: (*patiently bearing the burden of her husband's callousness*) Well, we must not snub the poor boy now, for I believe we shan't have him long among us. (*mournfully*) Anybody that looks in his face may see he's consumptive.

HARDCASTLE: (*drily*) Ay, if growing too fat be one of the symptoms.

MRS. HARDCASTLE: (*defensively*) He coughs sometimes.

HARDCASTLE: (*nodding vigorous agreement*) Yes, when his liquor goes the wrong way.

MRS. HARDCASTLE: (*despondently*) I'm actually afraid of his lungs.

HARDCASTLE: (*in hearty assent*) And truly, so am I; for he sometimes whoops like a speaking trumpet— (*A boisterous "halloo" is heard from the right.*) O there he goes—a very consumptive figure, truly.

---

[3] Archaic for "says she!"

Tony erupts from the left wings as if to race pell-mell across the stage. He is a short fat boy, wearing a scarlet jacket, a flowered silk waistcoat, buff breeches, and hunting boots. He is actually 21 years old but his dishevelled clothes and vacuous face give him the appearance of a spoiled brat. He pulls himself up short, snapping his hunting whip against his thigh, when his mother speaks.

MRS. HARDCASTLE: (*with saccharine endearment*) Tony, where are you going, my little charmer? (*cooing*) Won't you give papa and I a little of your company, lovey?

TONY: (*with brusque annoyance*) I'm in haste, mother; I cannot stay.

MRS. HARDCASTLE: (*taking him by the arm and examining his face with motherly concern*) You shan't venture out this raw evening, my dear; you look most shockingly.

TONY: (*impatiently attempting to pull away*) I can't stay, I tell you. The Three Pigeons expects me down every moment. There's some fun going forward.

HARDCASTLE: (*in self-confirmation*) Ay, the alehouse, the old place; I thought so.

MRS. HARDCASTLE: (*releasing Tony's arm sharply, in disgust*) A low, paltry set of fellows.

TONY: (*defensively*) Not so low neither. There's Dick Muggins the exciseman,[4] Jack Slang the horse doctor, little Aminadab that grinds the music box, and Tom Twist that spins the pewter platter.

MRS. HARDCASTLE: (*entreatingly and holding his arm again*) Pray, my dear, disappoint them for one night at least.

TONY: (*with a careless laugh*) As for disappointing *them*, I should not so much mind; but I can't abide to disappoint *myself*.

MRS. HARDCASTLE: (*still holding him by the arm*) You shan't go.

---

[4] Tax collector.

TONY: (*with unconcerned determination*) I will, I tell you.

MRS. HARDCASTLE: (*feebly*) I say you shan't.

TONY: (*with fiendish amusement*) We'll see which is the strongest, you or I. (*He throws the thong of his whip around her waist and drags her through the wings to the right.*)

HARDCASTLE: (*meditatively to himself*) Ay, there goes a pair that only spoil each other. But is not the whole age in a combination to drive sense and discretion out of doors? (*turning toward the left and seeing his daughter in the next room*) There's my pretty darling Kate; the fashions of the times have almost infected her too. By living a year or two in town, she is as fond of gauze, and French frippery, as the best of them. (*Kate Hardcastle enters from the left, looking very pert and extremely chic in her all-white lace trimmed dress*) Blessings on my pretty innocence! Dressed out as usual, my Kate. Goodness! what a quantity of superfluous silk hast thou got about thee, girl! I could never teach the fools of this age that the indigent world could be clothed out of the trimmings of the vain.

MISS HARDCASTLE: (*with good-humored matter-of-factness*) You know our agreement, sir. You allow me the morning to receive and pay visits, and to dress in my own manner; and in the evening, I put on my housewife's dress to please you.

HARDCASTLE: (*indulgently but admonishingly*) Well, remember I insist on the terms of our agreement; (*casually*) and, by the bye, I believe I shall have occasion to try your obedience this very evening.

MISS HARDCASTLE: (*with a suggestion of a pout*) I protest, sir, I don't comprehend your meaning.

HARDCASTLE: (*watching her closely to observe the effect of the startling news which he delivers in a very factual manner*) Then, to be plain with you, Kate, I expect the young gentleman I have chosen to be your

Then, to be plain with you, Kate, I expect the young gentleman I have chosen to be your husband from town this very day.

husband from town this very day. I have his father's letter, in which he informs me his son is set out, and that he intends to follow himself shortly after.

MISS HARDCASTLE: (*fluttering*) Indeed! I wish I had known something of this before. Bless me, how shall I behave? It's a thousand to one I shan't like him; our meeting will be so formal, and so like a thing of business, that I shall find no room for friendship or esteem.

HARDCASTLE: (*affectionately*) Depend upon it, child, I'll never control your choice; but Mr. Marlow, whom I have pitched upon, is the son of my old friend, Sir Charles Marlow, of whom you have heard me talk so often. The young gentleman has been bred a scholar, and is designed for an employment in the service of his country. I am told he's a man of an excellent understanding.

MISS HARDCASTLE: (*faintly*) Is he?

HARDCASTLE: (*encouragingly*) Very generous.

MISS HARDCASTLE: (*tentatively*) I believe I shall like him.

HARDCASTLE: (*slowly and thoughtfully*) Young and brave.

MISS HARDCASTLE: (*warming*) I'm sure I shall like him.

HARDCASTLE: (*as if adding an unimportant trifle*) And very handsome.

MISS HARDCASTLE: (*with gay impetuosity*) My dear papa, say no more, (*kissing his hand*), he's mine. (*abruptly*) I'll have him.

HARDCASTLE: (*enthusiastically*) And to crown all, Kate, he's one of the most bashful and reserved young fellows in all the world.

MISS HARDCASTLE: (*suddenly checking her gaiety*) Eh! you have frozen me to death again. The word *reserved* has undone all the rest of his accomplishments. A reserved lover, it is said, always makes a suspicious husband.

HARDCASTLE: (*with ponderous finality*) On the contrary, modesty seldom resides in a breast that is not enriched with nobler virtues. It was the very feature in his character that first struck me.

MISS HARDCASTLE: (*pertly*) He must have more striking features to catch me, I promise you. (*brightening again*) However, if he be so young, so handsome, and so everything as you mention, I believe he'll do still. (*airily*) I think I'll have him.

HARDCASTLE: (*teasingly*) Ay, Kate, but there is still an obstacle. It's more than an even wager, he may not have *you*.

MISS HARDCASTLE: (*pretending to be affronted*) My dear papa, why will you mortify one so? (*with self-confident unconcern*) Well, if he refuses, instead of breaking my heart at his indifference, I'll only break my glass for its flattery, set my cap to some newer fashion, and look out for some less difficult admirer.

HARDCASTLE: (*adoring his daughter's spirit as much as he does her beauty*) Bravely resolved! (*in good-humored anticipation*) In the meantime I'll go prepare the servants for his reception; as we seldom see company, they want as much training as a company of recruits the first day's muster. (*He goes off to left.*)

MISS HARDCASTLE: (*nervously to herself*) Lud, this news of papa's puts me all in a flutter. Young, handsome; these he put last, but I put them foremost. Sensible, good-natured; I like all that. But then, reserved and sheepish; that's much against him. (*frowning thoughtfully*) Yet can't he be cured of his timidity by being taught to be proud of his wife? (*brightening*) Yes, and can't I— (*checking her meditations with a laugh at her own expense*) But I vow I'm disposing of the husband, before I have secured the lover. (*During this last line, Miss Neville, only slightly less attractive but more serious and less volatile than her bosom friend, comes in from the outer door at the right. She wears a bonnet and a small cape which covers the upper part of her light blue dress. She is not given a chance to utter a word before Miss Hardcastle rushes forward to embrace her while speaking breathlessly.*)

I'm glad you're come, Neville, my dear. Tell me, Constance, how do I look this evening? (*moving back so that she can be fully seen*) Is there anything whimsical about me? Is it one of my well-looking days, child? Am I in face today?

MISS NEVILLE: (*reassuringly*) Perfectly, my dear. (*with mock seriousness, knowing her friend's flighty disposition*) Yet, now I look again—bless me!—sure, no accident has happened among the canary birds or the goldfishes? Has your brother or the cat been meddling? Or has the last novel been too moving?

MISS HARDCASTLE: (*disdainfully*) No; nothing of all this. (*dramatically*) I have been threatened—I can scarce get it out—I have been threatened with a lover.

MISS NEVILLE: (*flatly*) And his name—

MISS HARDCASTLE: (*making a revelation*) Is Marlow.

MISS NEVILLE: (*with sudden interest*) Indeed!

MISS HARDCASTLE: (*impressively*) The son of Sir Charles Marlow.

MISS NEVILLE: (*with great surprise*) As I live, the most intimate friend of Mr. Hastings, *my* admirer. They are never asunder. I believe you *must* have seen him when we lived in town.

MISS HARDCASTLE: Never.

MISS NEVILLE: (*thoughtfully but without priggish overtones*) He's a very singular character, I assure you. Among women of reputation and virtue, he is the modestest man alive; but his acquaintance give him a very different character among creatures of another stamp: you understand me.

MISS HARDCASTLE: (*catching the innuendo but exhibiting no particular prudery*) An odd character, indeed. I shall never be able to manage him. What shall I do? Pshaw, think no more of him, but trust to occurrences for success. (*more seriously*) But how goes on your own affair, my dear? Has my mother been courting you for by brother Tony, as usual?

MISS NEVILLE: (*sardonically*) I have just come from

one of our agreeable tête-à-têtes. She has been saying a hundred tender things, and setting off her pretty monster as the very pink of perfection.

MISS HARDCASTLE: (*confidentially*) And her partiality is such, that she actually thinks him so. A fortune like yours is no small temptation. Besides, as she has the sole management of it, I'm not surprised to see her unwilling to let it go out of the family.

MISS NEVILLE: (*deprecatingly*) A fortune like mine, which chiefly consists of jewels, is no such mighty temptation. But at any rate if my dear Hastings be but constant, I make no doubt to be too hard for her at last. However, I let her suppose that I am in love with her son, and she never once dreams that my affections are fixed upon another.

MISS HARDCASTLE: (*warmly*) My good brother holds out stoutly. I could almost love him for hating you so.

MISS NEVILLE: (*agreeing*) It is a good-natured creature at bottom, and I'm sure would wish to see me married to anybody but himself. (*The tinkling of a bell is heard in the distance.*) But my aunt's bell rings for our afternoon's walk round the improvements. *Allons.*[5] Courage is necessary, as our affairs are critical.

MISS HARDCASTLE: (*seizing the reference of "Allons" to forthcoming battle and capping it wryly with a parody of Falstaff's pre-battle remark to Prince Hal, "I would 'twere bedtime, Hal, and all well."*) Would it were bedtime and all were well. (*They go off together to the right to answer the summons of the bell.*)

Scene Two

The Pub or Public Room at the Three Pigeons, the local country tavern. At the rear toward the left is the bar and two settees, behind it a cupboard holding mugs, glasses, and assorted crockery. A heavy stone fireplace with its upward tapering chimney dominates the right side

---

[5] Opening word of the French national anthem and intended in the same way: "Onward!"

of the rear wall. In front of the fireplace but not too close to it for comfort, several young countrymen, dressed in slight variations of Tony's costume, lounge in abandoned attitudes around a large table, smoking churchwarden pipes and swilling punch from mugs which are replenished from a large punchbowl in the center of the table. Tony sits at the head of the table, his chair on a platform which raises him a little above the others, facing the audience. He holds his hunting whip in his hand and is obviously presiding over the ceremonies. The time is early evening, as indicated by the two lighted candles on the table, shortly after the preceding scene. General shouting and applause, presumably for a speech which has just concluded, is heard as the scene begins.

ALL: (*in confused miscellaneous noise-making*) Hurrea, hurrea, hurrea, bravo!

Tony pounds the table with his whip-stock, looking like an auctioneer knocking down an object at a sale. Partial order is restored.

FIRST FELLOW: Now gentlemen, silence for a song. The Squire is going to knock himself down for a song.

ALL: (*shouting drunkenly*) Ay, a song, a song!

TONY: (*happily pounding away again until the noise subsides*) Then I'll sing you, gentlemen, a song I made upon this alehouse, The Three Pigeons. (*He rises and sings the three stanzas; they all join in the chorus.*)

SONG

Let schoolmasters puzzle their brain,
  With grammar, and nonsense, and learning;
Good liquor, I stoutly maintain,
  Gives genius a better discerning.
Let them brag of their heathenish gods,
  Their Lethes, their Styxes, and Stygians,[1]

---

[1] Classical references to forgetfulness and death, followed by a Latin declension.

Their quis, and their quaes, and their quods,
    They're all but a parcel of pigeons.[2]
           Toroddle, toroddle, toroll.

When Methodist preachers come down,
    A-preaching that drinking is sinful,
I'll wager the rascals a crown,
    They always preach best with a skinful.
But when you come down with your pence,
    For a slice of their scurvy religion,
I'll leave it to all men of sense,
    But you my good friend are the pigeon.
           Toroddle, toroddle, toroll.

Then come, put the jorum[3] about,
    And let us be merry and clever,
Our hearts and our liquors are stout,
    Here's the Three Jolly Pigeons forever.
Let some cry up woodcock or hare,
    Your bustards, your ducks, and your widgeons;
But of all the birds in the air,
    Here's a health to the Three Jolly Pigeons.
           Toroddle, toroddle, toroll.

ALL: (*in drunken applause*) Bravo, bravo!

FIRST FELLOW: (*admiringly*) The Squire has got spunk in him.

SECOND FELLOW: (*enthusiastically*) I loves to hear him sing, bekeays he never gives us anything that's *low*.[4]

THIRD FELLOW: (*with intoxicated certainty*) O damn anything that's *low;* I cannot bear it.

FOURTH FELLOW: (*believing himself to be imitating the delicate accents of high society*) The genteel thing is

---

[2] Slang for "simpletons."

[3] The punch-bowl.

[4] A satiric reference to the genteel decorum of sentimental comedy which presented only the affluent and well-bred.

the genteel thing at any time; (*All nod thoughtful approval.*) if so be that a gentleman bees in a concatenation accordingly.[5]

THIRD FELLOW: (*responding in kind*) I like the maxum of it, Master Muggins. What though I am obligated to dance a bear, a man may be a gentleman for all that. May this be my poison (*holding up his mug*) if my bear ever dances but to the very genteelest of tunes: "Water Parted," or the Minuet in *Ariadne*.[6]

SECOND FELLOW: (*sighing lugubriously*) What a pity it is the Squire is not come to his own. It would be well for all the publicans[7] within ten miles round of him. (*All laugh.*)

TONY: (*vehemently*) Ecod and so it would, Master Slang. I'd then show what it was to keep choice of company.

SECOND FELLOW: (*in hearty approbation*) O he takes after his own father for that. To be sure, old Squire Lumpkin was the finest gentleman I ever set my eyes on. For winding the straight horn, or beating a thicket for a hare, or a wench, he never had his fellow. It was a saying in the place, that he kept the best horses, dogs, and girls in the whole county. (*All laugh.*)

TONY: (*largely*) Ecod, and when I'm of age I'll be no bastard, I promise you. I have been thinking of Bet Bouncer and the miller's gray mare to begin with. But come, my boys, drink about and be merry, for you pay no reckoning. (*The landlord comes in from the door at the right.*) Well, Stingo, what's the matter?

LANDLORD: There be two gentlemen in a post chaise at the door. They have lost their way upo' the forest; and they are talking something about Mr. Hardcastle.

TONY: (*slapping his thigh*) As sure as can be, one of

---

[5] He possibly means that a gentleman's parts are all of a piece by a kind of natural inevitability.

[6] "Water Parted," a song in Arne's opera *Artaxerxes; Ariadne*, an operetta by Handel.

[7] Tavern-keepers.

them must be the gentleman that's coming down to court my sister. Do they seem to be Londoners?

LANDLORD: I believe they may. They look woundily[8] like Frenchmen.

TONY: (*in a business-like way*) Then desire them to step this way, and I'll set them right in a twinkling. (*with a grimace at his drinking companions as the landlord goes out*) Gentlemen, as they mayn't be good enough company for you, step down for a moment, and I'll be with you in the squeezing of a lemon. (*to himself as his companions sidle out to the next room through the open wings to the left*) Father-in-law[9] has been calling me whelp, and hound, this half year. Now, if I pleased, I could be so revenged upon the old grumbletonian. But then I'm afraid—afraid of what? (*with reckless bravado*) I shall soon be worth fifteen hundred a year, and let him frighten me out of *that* if he can.

The landlord returns, directing Marlow and Hastings, both in riding costumes and carrying whips.

MARLOW: (*tired and annoyed*) What a tedious, uncomfortable day we had of it! We were told it was but forty miles across the country, and we have come about three-score.

HASTINGS: (*irritably*) And all, Marlow, from that unaccountable reserve of yours, that would not let us enquire more frequently on the way.

MARLOW: (*in an exasperated semblance of apology*) I own, Hastings, I am unwilling to lay myself under an obligation to everyone I meet, and often stand the chance of an unmannerly answer.

HASTINGS: (*looking squarely at Tony*) At present, however, we are not likely to receive *any* answer.

TONY: (*as if rousing from a stupor*) No offense, gentlemen. But I'm told you have been enquiring for one Mr. Hardcastle, in these parts. Do you know what part of the country you are in?

---
[8] Wonderfully.
[9] Stepfather.

HASTINGS: (*with tired civility*) Not in the least, sir, but should thank you for information.

TONY: (*slyly*) Nor the way you came?

HASTINGS: (*wearily*) No, sir; but if you can inform us—

TONY: (*cutting him off*) Why, gentlemen, if you know neither the road you are going, nor where you are, nor the road you came, the first thing I have to inform you is, (*profoundly*) that—you have lost your way.

MARLOW: (*disgustedly paraphrasing Horatio's remark to Hamlet*) We wanted no ghost to tell us that.

TONY: (*politely*) Pray, gentlemen, may I be so bold as to ask the place from whence you came?

MARLOW: (*gruffly*) That's not necessary towards directing us where we are to go.

TONY: (*soothingly*) No offence; but question for question is all fair, you know. Pray, gentlemen, is not this same Hardcastle a cross-grained, old-fashioned, whimsical fellow, with an ugly face, a daughter, and a pretty son?

HASTINGS: (*noncommittally*) We have not seen the gentleman, but he has the family you mention.

TONY: (*with enthusiasm*) The daughter, a tall, trapesing, trolloping, talkative maypole; the son, a pretty, well-bred, agreeable youth, that everybody is fond of.

MARLOW: (*coldly*) Our information differs in this. The daughter is said to be well-bred and beautiful; the son an awkward booby, reared up and spoiled at his mother's apron string.

TONY: (*giggling idiotically*) He-he-hem!—Then, gentlemen, all I have to tell you is, that you won't reach Mr Hardcastle's house this night, I believe.

HASTINGS: (*with gloomy resignation*) Unfortunate!

TONY: (*shaking his head*) It's a damned long, dark, boggy, dirty, dangerous way. (*winking slyly at the landlord*) Stingo, tell the gentlemen the way to Mr. Hardcastle's; Mr. Hardcastle's of Quagmire Marsh, (*winking again*) you understand me.

LANDLORD: (*playing along*) Master Hardcastle's! Lack-a-daisy, my masters, you're come a deadly deal wrong! When you came to the bottom of the hill, you should have crossed down Squash Lane.

MARLOW: (*with utter lack of comprehension*) Cross down Squash Lane!

LANDLORD: Then you were to keep straight forward, till you came to four roads.

MARLOW: (*dully as if reciting a meaningless piece by rote*) Come to where four roads meet!

TONY: (*sharply*) Ay; but you must be sure to take only one of them.

MARLOW: (*with glum disgust*) O sir, you're facetious.

TONY: (*rattling on*) Then keeping to the right, you are to go sideways till you come upon Crack-skull Common: there you must look sharp for the track of the wheel, and go forward, till you come to farmer Murrain's barn. Coming to the farmer's barn, you are to turn to the right, and then to the left, and then to the right about again, till you find out the old mill—

MARLOW: (*interrupting in utter bewilderment*) Zounds, man! we could as soon find out the longitude!

HASTINGS: What's to be done, Marlow?

MARLOW: (*looking around*) This house promises but a poor reception; though perhaps the landlord can accommodate us.

LANDLORD: (*quickly*) Alack, master, we have but one spare bed in the whole house.

TONY: (*even more quickly*) And to my knowledge that's taken up by three lodgers already. (*after a pause during which everyone seems completely at a loss*) I have hit it. Don't you think, Stingo, our landlady could accommodate the gentlemen by the fireside, with—three chairs and a bolster?

HASTINGS: (*testily*) I hate sleeping by the fireside.

MARLOW: (*irascibly*) And I detest your three chairs and a bolster.

TONY: (*with mock sympathy*) You do, do you?—
(*meditatively*) Then, let me see—what—if you go on a
mile further, to the Buck's Head; the old Buck's Head
on the hill, one of the best inns in the whole county?

HASTINGS: (*with vast relief*) O ho! so we have escaped
an adventure for this night, however.

LANDLORD: (*apart to Tony*) Sure, you ben't sending
them to your father's as an inn, be you?

TONY: (*apart to the landlord*) Mum, you fool you. Let
them find that out. (*aloud to Marlow and Hastings*) You
have only to keep on straight forward, till you come to a
large old house by the roadside. You'll see a pair of large
horns over the door. That's the sign. Drive up the yard,
and call stoutly about you.

HASTINGS: (*cheerfully*) Sir, we are obliged to you. The
servants can't miss the way?

TONY: (*helpfully*) No, no; but I tell you, though, the
landlord is rich, and going to leave off business; so he
wants to be thought a gentleman, saving your presence,
he! he! he! He'll be for giving you his company, and,
ecod, if you mind him, he'll persuade you that his mother
was an alderman and his aunt a justice of peace.

LANDLORD: (*chiming in*) A troublesome old blade, to
be sure; but a keeps as good wines and beds as any in the
whole country.

MARLOW: (*anxious to be off*) Well, if he supplies us
with these, we shall want no further connection. We are
to turn to the right, did you say?

TONY: (*insistently*) No, no; straight forward. I'll just
step myself, and show you a piece of the way. (*He waves
them through the door in front of him. Just before he
goes out, he turns to the landlord and holds a finger to
his lips*) Mum!

LANDLORD: (*as he turns toward the inner room to the
left*) Ah, bless your heart, for a sweet, pleasant—damn'd
mischievous son of a whore. (*He goes out.*)

ACT TWO

A return to the living room of the Hardcastle mansion. The time is early evening, immediately after the preceding scene. Hardcastle enters the room followed by four awkward servants who are dressed in footman's livery to which they are obviously unaccustomed. Their faces give an impression of vacuous bewilderment as these country louts are suddenly being pressed into an alien service.

HARDCASTLE: (*with the air of lord of the manor*) Well, I hope you're perfect in the table exercises I have been teaching you these three days. You all know your posts and your places, and can show that you have been used to good company, without ever stirring from home.

SERVANTS: (*lining up during Hardcastle's speech to present the appearance of an awkward squad and speaking in unison in flat, blank, uncomprehending, doltish voices*) Ay, ay.

HARDCASTLE: (*severely*) When company comes, you are not to pop out and stare, and then run in again, like frighted rabbits in a warren.

SERVANTS: (*with the same effect*) No, no.

HARDCASTLE: (*directing himself to the first servant who stands with his hands stiff at sides, thumbs turned out*) You, Diggory, whom I have taken from the barn, are to make a show at the side table; (*turning to the next*) and you, Roger, whom I have advanced from the plow, are to place yourself behind *my* chair. (*Roger beams with pride and shoves his hands casually into his pockets.*) Take your hands from your pockets, Roger. (*Startled, Roger pulls up his hands abruptly as if frightened so that they land just behind his ears at the back of his head*) And from your head, you blockhead, you. See how Diggory carries his hands. They're a little too stiff, indeed, but that's no great matter.

DIGGORY: (*loquaciously*) Ay, mind how I hold them. I learned to hold my hands this way when I was upon drill for the militia. And so being upon drill—

HARDCASTLE: (*cutting him off sharply*) You must not be so talkative, Diggory. You must be all attention to the guests. You must hear us talk, and not think of talking; you must see us drink, and not think of drinking; you must see us eat, and not think of eating.

DIGGORY: (*grinning idiotically*) By the laws, your worship, that's perfectly unpossible. Whenever Diggory sees yeating going forward, ecod, he's always wishing for a mouthful himself.

HARDCASTLE: (*with indulgent sternness*) Blockhead! Is not a bellyful in the kitchen as good as a bellyful in the parlor? Stay your stomach with that reflection.

DIGGORY: (*with humble gratitude*) Ecod, I thank your worship, I'll make a shift to stay my stomach with a slice of cold beef in the pantry.

HARDCASTLE: (*tolerantly*) Diggory, you are too talkative. Then if I happen to say a good thing, or tell a good story at table, you must not all burst out a-laughing, as if you made part of the company.

DIGGORY: (*with fatuous gratification*) Then, ecod, your worship must not tell the story of the Ould Grouse in the gun room; I can't help laughing at that—he! he! he!—for the soul of me. (*becoming more raucous with the memory*) We have laughed at that these twenty years—ha! ha! ha! (*Roger and Dick join uncertainly in the laughter.*)

HARDCASTLE: (*himself overcome*) Ha! ha! ha! The story is a good one. (*recovering himself*) Well, honest Diggory, you may laugh at that— (*Diggory and the others roar.*) but still remember to be attentive. (*They all close their mouths with a snap.*) Suppose one of the company should call for a glass of wine, how will you behave? (*He sits down at the table as if to dine and looks over his shoulder to Diggory*) A glass of wine, sir, if you please. (*They all stand as if petrified.*) Eh, why don't you move?

DIGGORY: (*placatingly*) Ecod, your worship, I never have courage till I see the eatables and drinkables brought upo' the table, and then I'm as bauld as a lion.

HARDCASTLE: (*exasperated*) What, will nobody move?

FIRST SERVANT: (*with stubborn stupidity*) I'm not to leave this pleace.

SECOND SERVANT: (*sullenly*) I'm sure it's no pleace of mine.

THIRD SERVANT: (*emphatically*) Nor mine, for sartain.

DIGGORY: (*with ultimate emphasis*) Wauns, and I'm sure it canna be mine.

HARDCASTLE: (*in hopeless rage*) You numbskulls! and so while, like your betters, you are quarreling for places, the guests must be starved. O you dunces! I find I must begin all over again (*hearing a noise outside*) But don't I hear a coach drive into the yard? (*peremptorily*) To your posts, you blockheads. (*brightening*) I'll go in the meantime and give my old friend's son a hearty reception at the gate. (*He goes off through the door at the right.*)

DIGGORY: (*shaking his head in dull puzzlement*) By the elevens, my pleace is gone quite out of my head.

ROGER: (*with a bewildered sigh*) I know that my pleace is to be everywhere.

FIRST SERVANT: (*in panic*) Where the devil is mine? (*He looks about hopelessly.*)

SECOND SERVANT: (*trembling with fright*) My pleace is to be nowhere at all; and so I'ze go about my business. (*He bolts offstage to the left. The others stand for a moment as if glued with terror to their places, then bolt off after him.*)

Scarcely a moment elapses when another servant enters

from the right door, carrying two silver candlesticks and ushering in Marlow and Hastings.

SERVANT: (*obsequiously*) Welcome, gentlemen, very welcome! This way.

HASTINGS: (*wearily*) After the disappointments of the day, welcome once more, Charles to the comforts of a clean room and a good fire. (*inspecting the room*) Upon my word, a very well-looking house; antique but creditable.

The servant places the candlesticks on the table and goes out through the right wings.

MARLOW: (*tired and out of spirits*) The usual fate of a large mansion. Having first ruined the master by good housekeeping, it at last comes to levy contributions as an inn.

HASTINGS: (*cynically agreeing*) As you say, we passengers are to be taxed to pay all these fineries. I have often seen a good sideboard or a marble chimney piece, though not actually put in the bill, inflame a reckoning confoundedly.

MARLOW: (*displaying his worldly wisdom about hotels in general*) Travelers, George, must pay in all places. The only difference is, that in good inns you pay dearly for luxuries; in bad inns, you are fleeced and starved.

HASTINGS: (*admiringly*) You have lived pretty much among them. (*wonderingly*) In truth, I have been often surprised, that you who have seen so much of the world, with your natural good sense, and your many opportunities, could never yet acquire a requisite share of assurance.

MARLOW: (*glumly*) The Englishman's malady. But tell me, George, where could I have learned that assurance you talk of? My life has been chiefly spent in a college or an inn, in seclusion from that lovely part of the creation that chiefly teach men confidence. I don't know that I was ever familiarly acquainted with a single modest woman—except my mother.— (*brightening*) But among females of another class, you know—

HASTINGS: (*interrupting with a laugh*) Ay, among them you are impudent enough, of all conscience.

MARLOW: (*offering his essential loneliness as explanation*) They are of *us,* you know.

HASTINGS: (*shaking his head*) But in the company of women of reputation I never saw such an idiot, such a trembler; you look for all the world as if you wanted an opportunity of stealing out of the room.

MARLOW: (*with forthright frankness*) Why, man, that's because I *do* want to steal out of the room. Faith, I have often formed a resolution to break the ice, and rattle away at any rate. But I don't know how, a single glance from a pair of fine eyes has totally overset my resolution. An impudent fellow may counterfeit modesty, but I'll be hanged if a modest man can ever counterfeit impudence.

HASTINGS: (*encouragingly*) If you could but say half the fine things to them that I have heard you lavish upon the barmaid of an inn, or even a college bed maker—

MARLOW: (*fatalistically*) Why, George, I *can't* say fine things to them. They freeze, they petrify me. They may talk of a comet, or a burning mountain, or some such bagateele. But to me, a modest woman, dressed out in all her finery, is the most tremendous object of the whole creation.

HASTINGS: (*despairing of him*) Ha! ha! ha! At this rate, man, how can you ever expect to marry!

MARLOW: (*with a wry smile*) Never, unless as among kings and princes, my bride were to be courted by proxy. If, indeed, like an Eastern bridegroom, one were to be introduced to a wife he never saw before, it might be endured. But to go through all the terrors of a formal courtship, together with the episode of aunts, grandmothers and cousins, and at last to blurt out the broad staring question of "Madam, will you marry me?" No, no, that's a strain much above me, I assure you.

HASTINGS: I pity you. (*quizzically*) But how do you intend behaving to the lady you are come down to visit at the request of your father?

MARLOW: (*with full consciousness of his social inepti-tude*) As I behave to all other ladies. Bow very low; answer yes or no to all her demands. But for the rest, I don't think I shall venture to look in her face, till I see my father's again.

HASTINGS: (*wonderingly and with a touch of admiration*) I'm surprised that one who is so warm a friend can be so cool a lover.

MARLOW: (*warmly*) To be explicit, my dear Hastings, my chief inducement down was to be instrumental in forwarding your happiness, not my own. Miss Neville loves you, the family don't know you, as my friend you are sure of a reception, and let honor do the rest.

HASTINGS: (*with equal warmth*) My dear Marlow! (*putting both hands on his shoulders*) But I'll suppress the emotion. Were I a wretch, meanly seeking to carry off a fortune, you should be the last man in the world I would apply to for assistance. But Miss Neville's person is all I ask, and that is mine, both from her deceased father's consent, and her own inclination.

MARLOW: (*with generous admiration*) Happy man! You have talents and art to captivate any woman. I'm doomed to adore the sex, and yet to converse with the only part of it I despise. (*lugubriously*) This stammer in my address, and this awkward unprepossessing, visage of mine, can never permit me to soar above the reach of a milliner's 'prentice, or one of the duchesses of Drury Lane.[1] (*seeing Hardcastle about to enter*) Pshaw! this fellow here to interrupt us.

HARDCASTLE: (*entering through the same door with his hands spread wide in a beaming welcome*) Gentlemen, once more you are heartily welcome. (*expansively*) Which is Mr. Marlow? (*Marlow nods in a distant fashion*) Sir, you're heartily welcome. (*convivially*) It's not my way, you see, to receive my friends with my back to

---

[1] Light-principled women of the theater district.

the fire. I like to give them a hearty reception in the old style at my gate. I like to see their horses and trunks taken care of.

MARLOW: (*aside to Hastings with an air of slight annoyance*) He has got our names from the servants already. (*to Hardcastle with cold civility*) We approve your caution and hospitality, sir. (*turning to Hastings to make it clear to Hardcastle that he is dismissed*) I have been thinking, George, of changing our traveling dresses in the morning. I am grown confoundedly ashamed of mine.

HARDCASTLE: (*ignoring the snub and acting as if Marlow were apologizing for not changing his clothes before dinner*) I beg, Mr. Marlow, you'll use no ceremony in this house.

HASTINGS: (*replying to George and completely ignoring Hardcastle's presence and his hospitable statement*) I fancy, Charles, you're right; the first blow is half the battle. (*with a slight flourish as he refers to the costume he intends to wear*) I intend opening the campaign with the white and gold.

HARDCASTLE: (*extremely puzzled, but determined to be gracious to his guests*) Mr. Marlow—Mr. Hastings— (*They seem to remain absorbed in their own thoughts.*) Gentlemen, pray be under no restraint in this house. This is Liberty Hall, gentlemen. You may do just as you please here.

MARLOW: (*continuing to ignore him*) Yet, George, if we open the campaign too fiercely at first, we may want ammunition before it is over. I think to reserve the embroidery to secure a retreat.

HARDCASTLE: (*seizing upon the military reference to launch into one of his favorite, even if inaccurate, reminiscences*) Your talking of a retreat, Mr. Marlow, puts me in mind of the Duke of Marlborough, when we went to besiege Denain. He first summoned the garrison—

MARLOW: (*rudely interrupting to discuss his gold*

waistcoat with Hastings) Don't you think the *ventre d'or* waistcoat will do with the plain brown?

HARDCASTLE: (*with determination*) He first summoned the garrison, which might consist of about five thousand men—

HASTINGS: (*shaking his head*) I think not: brown and yellow mix but very poorly.

HARDCASTLE: (*more loudly*) I say, gentlemen, as I was telling you, he summoned the garrison, which might consist of about five thousand men—

MARLOW: (*pensively, to Hastings*) The girls like finery.

HARDCASTLE: (*almost shouting*) Which might consist of about five thousand men, well appointed with stores, ammunition, and other implements of war. "Now," says the Duke of Marlborough to George Brooks, that stood next to him—you must have heard of George Brooks— "I'll pawn my dukedom," says he, "but I take that garrison without spilling a drop of blood." (*He has clearly captured the attention of the young men. He lowers his voice as if to proceed at a milder and more comfortable pace.*) So—

MARLOW: (*as if speaking to a feeble-minded inferior*) What, my good friend, if you gave us a glass of punch in the meantime; it would help us to carry on the siege with vigor.

HARDCASTLE: (*thoroughly shocked*) Punch, sir! (*aside*) This is the most unaccountable kind of modesty I ever met with.

MARLOW: (*patiently*) Yes, sir, punch. A glass of warm punch, after our journey, will be comfortable. (*betraying his amusement with this garrulous old simpleton*) This is Liberty Hall, you know.

HARDCASTLE: (*moving toward the table on which a bowl of claret-cup stands in readiness for the guests*) Here's cup, sir.

MARLOW: (*aside to Hastings as they follow him to-*

ward the table) So this fellow, in his Liberty Hall, will only let us have just what *he* pleases.

HARDCASTLE: (*filling three cups from the bowl*) I hope you'll find it to your mind. I have prepared it with my own hands, and I believe you'll own the ingredients are tolerable. (*Each picks up a cup.*) Will you be so good as to pledge me, sir? Here, Mr. Marlow, here is to our better acquaintance. (*drinks*)

MARLOW: (*aside*) A very impudent fellow this! But he's a character, and I'll humor him a little. (*with mock solemnity, to Hardcastle*) Sir, my service to you. (*drinks*)

HASTINGS: (*aside to Marlow*) I see this fellow wants to give us his company, and forgets that he's an innkeeper before he has learned to be a gentleman.

MARLOW: (*humoring the innkeeper*) From the excellence of your cup, my old friend, I suppose you have a good deal of business in this part of the country. Warm work, now and then, at elections, I suppose.

HARDCASTLE: (*naturally assuming that Marlow is referring to him as an electoral candidate who would distribute free refreshment to his constituents*) No, sir, I have long given that work over. Since our betters have hit upon the expedient of electing each other, there is no business "for us that sell ale."

HASTINGS: (*amused*) So, then you have no turn for politics, I find.

HARDCASTLE: (*contemptuously*) Not in the least. There was a time, indeed, I fretted myself about the mistakes of government, like other people; but finding myself every day grow more angry, and the government growing no better, I left it to mend itself. Since that, I no more trouble my head about *Heyder Ally,* or *Ally Cawn,* than about *Ally Croaker.*[2] (*drinking again*) Sir, my service to you.

---

[2] A rather clumsy attempt at humor, based on linking the three "Ally's": Haidar Ali, Sultan of Mysore; Ali Khan, Sultan of Bengal; and Ally Croaker whose name figured in a popular Irish song.

HASTINGS: (*oblivious to the joke*) So that with eating above stairs, and drinking below, with receiving your friends within, and amusing them without, you lead a good, pleasant, bustling life of it.

HARDCASTLE: (*warming to this recognition of his importance*) I do stir about a great deal, that's certain. Half the differences of the parish are adjusted in this very parlor.

MARLOW: (*drinking and smacking his lips*) And you have an argument in your cup, old gentleman, better than any in Westminster Hall.[3]

HARDCASTLE: (*pleased*) Ay, young gentleman, that, and a little philosophy.

MARLOW: (*aside to Hastings*) Well, this is the first time I ever heard of an innkeeper's philosophy.

HASTINGS: (*with genial condescension*) So then, like an experienced general, you attack them on every quarter. If you find their reason manageable, you attack it with your philosophy; if you find they have no reason, you attack them with this. (*raising his cup*) Here's your health, my philosopher. (*drinks*)

HARDCASTLE: (*in a mellow mood, feeling that he has been mistaken and that these are fine young gentlemen after all*) Good, very good, thank you; ha! ha! Your generalship puts me in mind of Prince Eugene, when he fought the Turks at the battle of Belgrade. You shall hear—

MARLOW: (*interrupting drily*) Instead of the battle of Belgrade, I believe it's almost time to talk about supper. What has your philosophy got in the house for supper?

HARDCASTLE: (*deeply affronted again*) For supper, sir! (*aside*) Was ever such a request to a man in his own house!

MARLOW: (*insistently*) Yes, sir, supper sir; I begin to feel an appetite. I shall make devilish work tonight in the larder, I promise you.

---

[3] London law court.

HARDCASTLE: (*aside*) Such a brazen dog sure never my eyes beheld. (*attempting desperately to remain civil, to Marlow*) Why, really, sir, as for supper, I can't well tell. My Dorothy, and the cook-maid, settle these things between them. I leave these kind of things entirely to them.

MARLOW: (*unwilling to put up with the innkeeper's quixotic behavior any longer*) You do, do you?

HARDCASTLE: Entirely. (*attempting to placate his rude young guests*) By the bye, I believe they are in actual consultation upon what's for supper this moment in the kitchen.

MARLOW: (*calmly exerting his rights as a patron of the hotel*) Then I beg they'll admit *me* as one of their privy council. It's a way I have got. When I travel, I always choose to regulate my own supper. Let the cook be called. (*realizing by Hardcastle's outraged expression that he ought to humor the old man*) No offense I hope, sir.

HARDCASTLE: (*too stunned to know really how to react and determined to abide by his own old-fashioned ideas of the laws of hospitality*) Oh, no, sir, none in the least; yet I don't know how; our Bridget, the cook-maid, is not very communicative upon these occasions. Should we send for her, she might scold us all out of the house.

HASTINGS: (*compromisingly*) Let's see your list of the larder, then. I ask it as a favor. I always match my appetite to my bill of fare. (*slapping him genially on the back*)

MARLOW: (*to Hardcastle who is momentarily speechless*) Sir, he's very right, and it's my way, too.

HARDCASTLE: (*recovering and unconsciously stating what will only continue the delusion*) Sir, you have a right to command here. (*calling to a servant*) Here, Roger, bring us the bill of fare for tonight's supper; I believe it's drawn out. (*with attempted joviality, to Hastings*) Your manner, Mr. Hastings, puts me in mind of my uncle, Colonel Wallop. It was a saying of his that no man was sure of his supper till he had eaten it.

HASTINGS: (*aside to Marlow while Roger brings a slip of paper to Hardcastle who hands it to Marlow*) All upon the high ropes! His uncle a colonel! We shall soon hear of his mother being a justice of peace.

MARLOW: (*perusing the paper*) What's here? For the first course; for the second course; for the dessert. (*to Hardcastle*) The devil, sir, do you think we have brought down the whole Joiners' Company, or the Corporation of Bedford,[4] to eat up such a supper? (*off-handedly*) Two or three things, clean and comfortable, will do.

HASTINGS: (*curious*) But let's hear it.

MARLOW: (*reading*) For the first course, at the top, a pig, and prune sauce.

HASTINGS: (*gloriously unaware of the old gentleman who had hoped the menu would please them*) Damn your pig, I say!

MARLOW: (*emphatically*) And damn your prune sauce, say I!

HARDCASTLE: (*apologetically*) And yet, gentlemen, to men that are hungry, pig with prune sauce is very good eating.

MARLOW: (*ignoring him and continuing to read*) At the bottom, a calf's tongue and brains.

HASTINGS: (*to Hardcastle, giving an impression of the extreme of rudeness but intending only that he does not care to order this dish*) Let your brains be knocked out, my good sir; I don't like them.

MARLOW: (*casually and without any sense of the implications of his friend's remark*) Or you may clap them on a plate by themselves. *I* do.

HARDCASTLE: (*aside*) Their impudence confounds me. (*attempting to control himself*) Gentlemen, you are my guests; make what alterations you please. (*with heavy irony*) Is there anything else you wish to retrench or alter, gentlemen?

---

[4] The woodworkers guild or the officials of Bedford.

MARLOW: (*continuing to read the extensive menu*) Item: a pork pie, a boiled rabbit and sausages, a florentine, a shaking pudding, and a dish of tiff—(*having difficulty in making out the name of this elaborate delicacy*)—taff—taffety cream!

HASTINGS: (*expressing his provincial distrust of foreign concoctions*) Confound your made dishes! I shall be as much at a loss in this house as at a green and yellow dinner at the French ambassador's table. I'm for plain eating.

HARDCASTLE: (*utterly defeated but with growing irritation*) I'm sorry, gentlemen, that I have nothing you like; but if there be anything you have a particular fancy to—

MARLOW: (*aware from his extensive travels of the extraordinary quality of this bill-of-fare*) Why, really, sir, your bill of fare is so exquisite, that any one part of it is full as good as another. (*pleasantly but abruptly as to a servant*) Send us what you please. (*expeditiously*) So much for supper. And now to see that our beds are aired, and properly taken care of.

HARDCASTLE: (*politely but firmly*) I entreat you'll leave all that to me. You shall not stir a step.

MARLOW: (*implying the preposterousness of Hardcastle's remark*) Leave that to you! I protest, sir, you must excuse me; I *always* look to these things myself.

HARDCASTLE: (*with great definiteness*) I must *insist*, sir, you'll make yourself easy on that head.

MARLOW: (*heading toward the wings to the left, presumably leading inside since it is opposite the outer door through which they had entered*) You see I'm resolved on it. (*aside as he goes out*) A very troublesome fellow this, as ever I met with.

HARDCASTLE: (*striding after him*) Well, sir, I'm resolved at least to attend you. (*aside as he follows Marlow offstage*) This may be modern modesty, but I never saw anything look so like old-fashioned impudence.

HASTINGS: (*alone and musing to himself*) So I find

this fellow's civilities begin to grow troublesome. But who can be angry at those assiduities which are meant to please him? (*He pauses and looks about as if to examine the room. He startles suddenly as he catches sight of Miss Neville about to come into the room through the wings to the right.*) Ha! what do I see? (*going toward her as she enters*) Miss Neville, by all that's happy!

MISS NEVILLE: (*delighted*) My dear Hastings! (*They embrace.*) To what unexpected good fortune, to what accident, am I to ascribe this happy meeting?

HASTINGS: (*returning the warmth of her greeting*) Rather let me ask the same question, as I could never have hoped to meet my dearest Constance at an inn.

MISS NEVILLE: (*puzzled*) An inn! Sure you mistake! My aunt, my guardian, lives here. (*unbelievingly*) What could induce you to think this house an inn?

HASTINGS: (*equally puzzled*) My friend, Mr. Marlow, with whom I came down, and I have been sent here as to an inn, I assure you. A young fellow whom we accidentally met at a house hard by directed us hither.

MISS NEVILLE: (*very much amused*) Certainly it must be one of my hopeful cousin's tricks, of whom you have heard me talk so often; ha! ha! ha! ha!

HASTINGS: (*jealously*) He whom your aunt intends for you? He of whom I have such just apprehensions?

MISS NEVILLE: (*soothingly*) You have nothing to fear from him, I assure you. You'd adore him if you knew how heartily he despises me. (*confidentially*) My aunt knows it too, (*laughing at the absurdity*) and has undertaken to court me for him, and actually begins to think she has made a conquest.

HASTINGS: (*adoringly*) Thou dear dissembler! You must know, my Constance, I have just seized this happy opportunity of my friend's visit here to get admittance into the family. The horses that carried us down are now fatigued with their journey, but they'll soon be refreshed; (*with eager excitement*) and then, if my dearest girl will

*Leave that to you! I protest, sir, you must
excuse me; I always look to these things myself.*

trust in her faithful Hastings, we shall soon be landed in France, where even among slaves the laws of marriage are respected.[5]

MISS NEVILLE: (*restraining him*) I have often told you, that though ready to obey you, I yet should leave my little fortune behind with reluctance. The greatest part of it was left me by my uncle, the India director,[6] and chiefly consists in jewels. I have been for some time persuading my aunt to let me wear them. I fancy I'm very near succeeding. The instant they are put into my possession you shall find me ready to make them and myself yours. (*She curtsies low; he bows in acknowledgment.*)

HASTINGS: (*impatiently and with romantic superiority to property*) Perish the baubles! Your person is all I desire. (*suddenly remembering Marlow's character and situation*) In the meantime, my friend Marlow must not be let into his mistake. I know the strange reserve of his temper is such, that if abruptly informed of it, he would instantly quit the house before our plan was ripe for execution.

MISS NEVILLE: (*remonstrating*) But how shall we keep him in the deception? Miss Hardcastle is just returned from walking; what if we still continue to deceive him? (*looking nervously about and glimpsing Marlow about to return*) This, this way— (*She pulls Hastings to the corner of the room farthest from the wings through which Marlow now enters.*)

MARLOW: (*expecting to find Hastings where he left him and talking to him as he comes in without being fully conscious that he is off in a corner with a young lady*) The assiduities of these good people tease me beyond bearing. My host seems to think it ill manners to leave me alone, and so he claps not only himself but his old-fashioned wife on my back. They talk of coming to sup with us too;

---

[5] A topical reference to the Marriage Act of 1772 which required the King's consent to all marriages of state.

[6] A director of the East India Company.

and then, I suppose, we are to run the gauntlet through all the rest of the family. (*emerging from his annoyed self-preoccupation and suddenly conscious of the couple in the corner*) What have we got here? (*surmising that Hastings has acquired a fast lady*)

HASTINGS: (*in high spirits*) My dear Charles! Let me congratulate you! The most fortunate accident! Who do you think is just alighted?

MARLOW: (*noncommittally*) Cannot guess.

HASTINGS: (*enthusiastically*) Our mistresses, boy, Miss Hardcastle and Miss Neville. (*leading Miss Neville forward*) Give me leave to introduce Miss Constance Neville to your acquaintance (*continuing with glib invention after Marlow's bow and her curtsey*) Happening to dine in the neighborhood, they called on their return to take fresh horses here. Miss Hardcastle has just stepped into the next room, and will be back in an instant. (*attempting to impart his excitement*) Wasn't it lucky? eh!

MARLOW: (*to himself*) I have just been mortified enough of all conscience, and here comes something to complete my embarrassment.

HASTINGS: (*urgently*) Well! but wasn't it the most fortunate thing in the world?

MARLOW: (*in violent agitation*) Oh, yes. Very fortunate —a most joyful encounter—(*quivering with nervousness in the presence of Miss Neville*) But our dresses, George, you know, are in disorder— What if we postpone the happiness till tomorrow?—tomorrow at her own house— It will be every bit as convenient—and rather more respectful— (*with quick resolution and eyeing the door as if to make an abrupt exit*) Tomorrow let it be. (*making as if to leave*)

HASTINGS: (*sharply and authoritatively as he forcibly steps between Marlow and the door*) By no means, sir. Your ceremony will displease her. This disorder of your dress will show the ardor of your impatience. Besides, she knows you are in the house, and will permit you to see her.

MARLOW: (*a pathetic figure, nearly frantic, stammering with dry-throated helplessness*) O! the devil! how shall I support it? Hem! hem! Hastings, you must not go. You are to assist me, you know. I shall be confoundedly ridiculous. (*with the air of a condemned criminal*) Yet, hang it, I'll take courage! Hem!

HASTINGS: (*with amused encouragement*) Pshaw, man! it's but the first plunge, and all's over! She's but a woman, you know.

MARLOW: (*heaving a prodigious sigh*) And of all women, she that I dread most to encounter!

Miss Hardcastle enters, dressed in all the finery she is permitted (in accordance with her agreement with her father) to wear in the daytime. Having just come from a walk, she still carries a frilly parasol in her left daintily-gloved hand. A stunningly becoming bonnet is drawn down on either side of her face as if to emphasize the beauty of her features whose prim demureness, prepared for the occasion, is betrayed by her coquettish and faintly mischievous eyes. To receive this effect, one must look directly at her, as the audience is permitted to do. Marlow who never allows himself more than an occasional terrified sidelong squint, actually sees no more than her bonnet and the rest of her costume.

HASTINGS: (*attempting to introduce her*) Miss Hardcastle, Mr. Marlow, I'm proud of bringing two persons of such merit together, that only want to know, to esteem each other. (*She curtsies graciously; he bows vaguely in her general direction.*)

MISS HARDCASTLE: (*to herself*) Now, for meeting my modest gentleman with a demure face, and quite in his own manner. (*There is an awkward pause during which she is plainly waiting for him to acknowledge the introduction. He fidgets, wets his lips, seems on the verge of saying something, but no sound comes from him. She finally breaks the silence with quiet civility.*) I'm glad of your safe arrival, sir—I'm told you had some accidents by the way.

MARLOW: (*stammering and looking everywhere but in her direction*) Only a few, madam. Yes, we had some. Yes, madam, a good many accidents, but should be sorry —(*seems about to collapse*)—madam—or rather glad of any accidents—(*pulling himself together for a rapid, triumphant, though hoarse, ending*)—that are so agreeably concluded. Hem!

HASTINGS: (*aside to him*) You never spoke better in your whole life. Keep it up, and I'll insure you the victory.

MISS HARDCASTLE: (*modestly*) I'm afraid you flatter, sir. You that have seen so much of the finest company can find little entertainment in an obscure corner of the country.

MARLOW: (*gathing courage but still not daring to look directly at her*) I have lived, indeed, in the world, madam; but I have kept very little company. I have been but an observer upon life, madam, while others were enjoying it.

MISS NEVILLE: (*with simple earnestness*) But that, I am told, is the way to enjoy it at last.

HASTINGS: (*aside to Marlow*) Cicero never spoke better. Once more, and you are confirmed in assurance forever.

MARLOW: (*in a nervous aside to Hastings*) Hem! stand by me then, and when I'm down, throw in a word or two to set me up again.

MISS HARDCASTLE: (*with gentle encouragement*) An observer, like you, upon life, were, I fear, disagreeably employed, since you must have had much more to censure than to approve.

MARLOW: (*with forced bravado*) Pardon me, madam. I was always willing to be amused. The folly of most people is rather an object of mirth than uneasiness.

HASTINGS: (*aside to Marlow*) Bravo, bravo. Never spoke so well in your whole life. (*with genial casualness to Miss Hardcastle*) Well! Miss Hardcastle, I see that you and Mr. Marlow are going to be very good company. (*looking at Miss Neville*) I believe our being here will but embarrass the interview.

MARLOW: (*emphatically*) Not in the least, Mr. Hastings. We like your company of all things. (*frantically aside to him as Miss Neville nods and starts to leave the room*) Zounds! George, sure you won't go? How can you leave us?

HASTINGS: (*firmly*) Our presence will but spoil conversation, so we'll retire to the next room. (*aside to Marlow as he follows Miss Neville out to left*) You don't consider, man, that we are to manage a little *tête-à-tête* of our own.

Marlow, embarrassed and furtive, looks like a man who has been caught breaking open a church poor box and stands on the brink of disaster. There is a painful pause during which Miss Hardcastle looks curiously at his distraught maneuverings. With eyes steadfastly diverted, he sits down near the table, is aware that she is left standing, gets up in agitation, picks up another chair and places it between the fireplace and the table, vaguely indicating that it is intended for her. As she seats herself, he retreats to his own chair by the table, whereupon she moves her chair close to but slightly behind his and sits down again. She finally attempts to pick up the threads of the conversation.

MISS HARDCASTLE: (*attempting a sprightly manner*) But you have not been wholly an observer, I presume, sir. (*with sly archness*) The ladies, I shall hope, have employed some part of your addresses.

MARLOW: (*completely destroyed by this frontal attack*) Pardon me, madam, I—I—I—as yet—have studied —only—to—deserve them. (*He shivers with exhaustion from the supreme effort which this stammering speech cost him.*)

MISS HARDCASTLE: (*flirtatiously*) And *that,* some say, is the very worst way to obtain them.

MARLOW: (*looking yearningly toward the left wings through which his friend has departed*) Perhaps so, madam. But I love to converse only with the more grave and sensible part of the sex. (*making as if to rush off after Hastings*) But I'm afraid I grow tiresome.

MISS HARDCASTLE: (*gently but with great firmness*) Not at all sir; there is nothing I like so much as grave conversation myself; I could hear it forever. Indeed I have often been surprised how a man of *sentiment* could ever admire those light airy pleasures, where nothing reaches the heart.

MARLOW: (*hardly knowing what he is saying*) It's—a disease—of the mind, madam. In the variety of tastes there must be some who, wanting a relish—for—um—a —um—

MISS HARDCASTLE: (*ignoring his stammering and as if coaching a young pupil*) I understand you, sir. There must be some who, wanting[7] a relish for refined pleasures, pretend to despise what they are incapable of tasting.

MARLOW: (*still floundering*) My meaning, madam, but infinitely better expressed. (*He draws a deep breath.*) And I can't help observing—a— (*He goes completely to pieces and sits mutely observing his boots.*)

MISS HARDCASTLE: (*aside*) Who could ever suppose this fellow impudent upon some occasions. (*directly to him*) You were going to observe, sir,——

MARLOW: (*squirming painfully*) I was observing, madam— (*in frank defeat*) I protest, madam, I forget what I was going to observe.

MISS HARDCASTLE: (*in an amused aside*) I vow and so do I. (*encouragingly to him*) You were observing, sir, that in this age of hypocrisy—something about hypocrisy, sir.

---

[7] Lacking.

MARLOW: (*with a dry throat, his head bowed and turned away*) Yes, madam. In this age of hypocrisy there are few who, upon strict inquiry, do not—a—a—

MISS HARDCASTLE: (*with mock solemnity*) I understand you perfectly, sir.

MARLOW: (*aside*) Egad! and that's more than I do myself!

MISS HARDCASTLE: (*firmly*) You mean that in this hypocritical age there are few who do not condemn in public what they practice in private, and think they pay every debt to virtue when they praise it.

MARLOW: (*slightly recovering*) True, madam; those who have most virtue in their mouths have least of it in their bosoms. (*looking beseechingly for help toward the other room again*) But I'm sure I tire you, madam.

MISS HARDCASTLE: (*as if meaning deeply every word she says*) Not in the least, sir; there's something so agreeable and *spirited* in your manner, such *life* and *force*—pray, sir, go on.

MARLOW: (*like a chastised schoolboy*) Yes, madam. Morally speaking, madam— (*darting another wildly despairing glance toward the next room*) But I see Miss Neville expecting us in the next room. (*leaping to his feet with a sideways squint at Miss Hardcastle*) I would not intrude for the world.

MISS HARDCASTLE: (*with determination*) I protest, sir, I never was more agreeably entertained in all my life. Pray go on.

MARLOW: (*shuddering*) Yes, madam, I was— (*sits down again and turns a beseeching gaze towards the left*) But she *beckons* us to join her. (*jumping to his feet again*) Madam, shall I do myself the honor to attend you?

MISS HARDCASTLE: (*releasing him at last*) Well, then, I'll follow.

MARLOW: (*in a sardonic aside as he retreats from the room*) This pretty, smooth dialogue has done for me.

MISS HARDCASTLE: (*following his departure with her eyes and bursting into laughter when he is completely off-stage*) Ha! ha! ha! Was there ever such a sober, sentimental interview? I'm certain he scarce looked in my face the whole time. (*turning to a more thoughtful mood*) Yet the fellow, but for his unaccountable bashfulness, is pretty well, too. He has good sense, but then so buried in his fears, that it fatigues one more than ignorance. (*musing*) If I could teach him a little confidence, it would be doing somebody that I know of a piece of service. (*with a momentary blush as if being accused of designing a plan to make herself Mrs. Marlow*) But who is that somebody? (*with an airy self-conscious laugh as she exits to the right*) That, faith, is a question I can scarce answer.

Tony now enters from the left pursued by Miss Neville. Mrs. Hardcastle (now wearing a grotesquely elaborate headdress and otherwise gotten up in the height of poor taste) and Hastings, talking quietly, stroll on after them during their opening speeches.

TONY: (*with irritation*) What do you follow me for, cousin Con? I wonder you're not ashamed to be so very engaging.

MISS NEVILLE: (*flirtatiously*) I hope, cousin, one may speak to one's own relations, and not be to blame.

TONY: (*sullenly*) Ay, but I know what sort of a relation you want to make me though; but it won't do. I tell you, cousin Con, it won't do, so I beg you'll keep your distance. I want no nearer relationship.

She remains persistent and coquettes him to the back of the stage as the other couple's conversation becomes audible to the audience.

MRS. HARDCASTLE: (*gushingly*) Well! I vow, Mr. Hastings, you are very entertaining. There's nothing in the world I love to talk of so much as London, and the fashions, though I was never there myself.

HASTINGS: (*with mock incredulity*) Never there! You amaze me! From your air and manner, I concluded you

had been bred all your life either at Ranelagh, St. James's,
or Tower Wharf.[8]

MRS. HARDCASTLE: (*in a glow of delight*) O! sir, you're
only pleased to say so. We country persons can have no
manner at all. I'm in love with the town, and that serves
to raise me above some of our neighboring rustics; but
who can have a manner that has never seen the Pantheon,
the Grotto Gardens, the Borough, and such places, where
the nobility chiefly resort?[9] All I can do is to enjoy London at secondhand. I take care to know every *tête-à-tête*
from the *Scandalous Magazine,*[10] and have all the fashions, as they come out, in a letter from the two Miss
Ricketts of Crooked Lane. Pray how do you like this
head,[11] Mr. Hastings?

HASTINGS: (*pretending to be lost in admiration*) Extremely elegant and *dégagée,* upon my word, madam.
Your *friseur* is a Frenchman, I suppose?[12]

MRS. HARDCASTLE: (*blushing with pleasure*) I protest
I dressed it myself from a print in the *Ladies Memoran-
dum-book* for the last year.

HASTINGS: (*adding to the grossness of his flattery because of her failure to understand the full implications of
his remarks*) Indeed! Such a head in a side box, at the

---

[8] He is taking advantage of her ignorance to make fun of her,
by linking two highly fashionable places with a slum district.

[9] The nobility who did frequent the recently opened Pantheon
would never go near the popular Grotto Gardens in Southwark
Borough.

[10] Begun in 1769, the *Tête-à-Tête* was an ingenious monthly
feature of the *Town and Country Magazine* in which a sketch of
two socially prominent individuals was followed by an imaginary
conversation between them suggesting a scandalous and fashionable intrigue.

[11] The elaborate headdresses of the period were built on a wire
frame and were taken off when milady was not fashionably
dressed.

[12] Mrs. Hardcastle may or may not know enough common-
place French terms used in English to recognize *dégagée*—"sophisticated" and *friseur*—"hairdresser."

playhouse, would draw as many gazers as my Lady Mayoress at a city ball.

MRS. HARDCASTLE: (*with naïve frankness*) I vow, since inoculation began, there is no such thing to be seen as a plain woman;[13] so one must dress a little particular or one may escape in the crowd.

HASTINGS: (*with a low bow*) But that can never be your case, madam, in any dress.

MRS. HARDCASTLE: (*peevishly*) Yet, what signifies *my* dressing, when I have such a piece of antiquity by my side as Mr. Hardcastle? All I can say will never argue down a single button from his clothes. I have often wanted him to throw off his great flaxen wig and where he was bald to plaster it over, like my Lord Pately, with powder.

HASTINGS: (*agreeably*) You are right, madam; for, as among the ladies there are none ugly, so among the men there are none old.

MRS. HARDCASTLE: But what do you think his answer was? (*with scorn applicable to a barbarian*) Why, with his usual Gothic vivacity, he said I only wanted him to throw off his wig to convert it into a *tête*[14] for my own wearing.

HASTINGS: (*pretending to be shocked*) Intolerable! (*continuing his unperceived badinage*) At your age you may wear what you please, and it *must* become you.

MRS. HARDCASTLE: (*innocently*) Pray, Mr. Hastings, what do you take to be the most fashionable age about town?

HASTINGS: (*with outrageous flattery*) Some time ago, forty was all the mode; but I'm told the ladies intend to bring up fifty for the ensuing winter.

---

[13] The introduction of inoculation against smallpox early in the 18th century had steadily reduced the number of pock-marked feminine faces in England.

[14] The common term for an eighteenth century "head" or head-dress.

MRS. HARDCASTLE: (*transported*) Seriously? (*with a silly giggle*) Then I shall be too young for the fashion.

HASTINGS: (*airily but eyeing her sharply as he edges toward the subject of Miss Neville's inheritance*) No lady begins now to put on jewels till she's past forty. For instance, Miss there, (*indicating Miss Neville*) in a polite circle, would be considered as a child, as a mere maker of samplers.

MRS. HARDCASTLE: (*shaking her head*) And yet, Mistress Niece there thinks herself as much a woman, and is as fond of jewels as the oldest of us all.

HASTINGS: (*with a blatant pretense of innocence*) Your niece, is she? And that young gentleman—(*indicating Tony*) a *brother* of yours, I should presume?

MRS. HARDCASTLE: (*softly as she blushingly lowers her eyes*) My son, sir. They are contracted to each other. (*coyly*) Observe their little sports. They fall in and out ten times a day, as if they were man and wife already. (*raising her voice and calling to Tony*) Well, Tony, child, what soft things are you saying to your cousin Constance this evening?

TONY: (*belligerently*) I have been saying no soft things; but that it's very hard to be followed about so. Ecod! I've not a place in the house now that's left to myself but the stable. (*Tony and Miss Neville come forward.*)

MRS. HARDCASTLE: Never mind him, Con, my dear. He's in another story behind your back.

MISS NEVILLE: (*indulgently*) There's something generous in my cousin's manner. He falls out before faces to be forgiven in private.

TONY: (*about to call his mother a liar but recollecting himself in front of company*) That's a damned confounded—crack.

MRS. HARDCASTLE: (*blissfully ignorant*) Ah, he's a sly one! Don't you think they're like each other about the mouth, Mr. Hastings? The Blenkinsop mouth to a T. They're of a size, too. (*fatuously to Tony and Miss*

Neville) Back to back, my pretties, that Mr. Hastings
may see you. (*Miss Neville dutifully stands sideways.
Tony glares at his mother.*) Come Tony.

TONY: (*with a surly growl as he backs up to Miss
Neville and strikes his head against hers on his conclud-
ing words*) You had as good not make me, I tell you.

MISS NEVILLE: (*jumping away*) O lud! he has almost
cracked my head.

MRS. HARDCASTLE: (*indulgently reproving*) O the
monster! For shame, Tony. You a man, and behave so!

TONY: (*muttering sullenly*) If I'm a man, let me have
my fortin. Ecod! I'll not be made a fool of no longer.

MRS. HARDCASTLE: (*whimpering*) Is this, ungrateful
boy, all that I'm to get for the pains I have taken in your
education? I that have rocked you in your cradle, and
fed that pretty mouth with a spoon! Did I not work that
waistcoat to make you genteel? Did I not prescribe for
you every day, and weep while the receipt was operating?

TONY: (*harshly*) Ecod! you had reason to weep, for
you have been dosing me ever since I was born. I have
gone through every receipt in *The Complete Huswife* ten
times over; and you have thoughts of coursing me through
Quincy[15] next spring. (*angrily*) But, ecod! I tell you, I'll
not be made a fool of no longer.

MRS. HARDCASTLE: (*between anger and tears*) Wasn't
it all for your good, viper? Wasn't it all for your good?

TONY: (*peevishly*) I wish you'd let me and my good
alone, then. Snubbing this way when I'm in spirits! If
I'm to have any good, let it come of itself; not to keep
dinging it, dinging it into one so.

MRS. HARDCASTLE: (*reproachfully*) That's false; I
never see you when you're in spirits. No, Tony, you then

---

[15] Dr. John Quincy's *Complete English Dispensatory,* a book
for home medication, had many more "receipts" or remedies in it
than were contained in *The Complete Huswife* which was a general and comprehensive guide for the housewife.

go to the alehouse or kennel. I'm never to be delighted with your agreeable wild notes, unfeeling monster!

TONY: (*with a contemptuous laugh*) Ecod! mamma, your own notes are the wildest of the two.

MRS. HARDCASTLE: (*pitiably to Hastings*) Was ever the like? But I see he wants to break my heart, I see he does.

HASTINGS: (*unctiously*) Dear madam, permit me to lecture the young gentleman a little. I'm certain I can persuade him to his duty.

MRS. HARDCASTLE: (*with a sigh*) Well! I must retire. (*to Miss Neville*) Come, Constance, my love. (*tremulously to Hastings*) You see, Mr. Hastings, the wretchedness of my situation. Was ever poor woman so plagued with a dear, sweet, provoking, undutiful boy? (*She puts her arm around Miss Neville's waist and leads her offstage to the left.*)

TONY: (*bursting raucously into song the moment they leave*)

> There was a young man riding by,
> And fain would have his will.
> Rang do didlo dee.

(*stops abruptly and turns sharply to Hastings*) Don't mind her. Let her cry. It's the comfort of her heart. I have seen her and sister cry over a book for an hour together, and they said they liked the book the better the more it made them cry.

HASTINGS: (*amicably*) Then you're no friend to the ladies, I find, my pretty young gentleman?

TONY: (*grumpily*) That's as I find 'um.

HASTINGS: (*pointedly*) Not to her of your mother's choosing, I dare answer. (*as if weighing his impression of Miss Neville*) And yet she appears to me a pretty, well-tempered girl.

TONY: That's because you don't know as well as I. (*venomously*) Ecod! I know every inch about her; and there's not a more bitter cantankerous toad in all Christendom.

HASTINGS: (*aside*) Pretty encouragement this for a lover!

TONY: (*continuing*) I have seen her since the height of that. (*holding his hand below his waist*) She has as many tricks as a hare in a thicket, or a colt the first day's breaking.

HASTINGS: (*thoughtfully*) To me she appears sensible and silent!

TONY: (*snorting*) Ay, before company. But when she's with her playmates, she's as loud as a hog in a gate.

HASTINGS: (*argumentatively*) But there is a meek modesty about her that charms me.

TONY: Yes, but curb her never so little, she kicks up, and you're flung in a ditch.

HASTINGS: (*with earnestness*) Well, but you *must* allow her a little beauty.—Yes, you must allow her some beauty.

TONY: (*contemptuously implying that her beauty is artificial*) Bandbox! She's all a made-up thing, mun. (*his eyes lighting enthusiastically*) Ah! could you but see Bet Bouncer of these parts, you might then talk of beauty. Ecod, she has two eyes as black as sloes, and cheeks as broad and red as a pulpit cushion. She'd make two of she.

HASTINGS: (*confidentially, man-to-man*) Well, what say you to a friend that would take this bitter bargain off your hands?

TONY: (*not believing his ears*) Anon.

HASTINGS: (*repeating plainly*) Would you thank him that would take Miss Neville and leave you to happiness and your dear Betsy?

TONY: (*incredulously*) Ay; but where is there such a friend, for who would take *her*?

HASTINGS: (*in a conspiratorial manner*) I am he. If you but assist me, I'll engage to whip her off to France, and you shall never hear more of her.

TONY: (*shouting with joy*) Assist you! Ecod I will, to the last drop of my blood. I'll clap a pair of horses to your chaise that shall trundle you off in a twinkling, and maybe get you a part of her fortin besides, in jewels, that you little dream of.

HASTINGS: (*bowing to him*) My *dear* Squire, *this* looks like a lad of spirit.

TONY: (*grabbing him fraternally by the arm and leading him off to right*) Come along then, and you shall see more of my spirit before you have done with me. (*singing boisterously as they leave the stage together*)

> We are the boys
> That fears no noise
> Where the thundering cannons roar.

ACT THREE

The same, about three hours later. Hardcastle enters from the left, musing to himself.

HARDCASTLE: (*in an outraged tone*) What could my old friend Sir Charles mean by recommending his son as the modestest young man in town? To me he appears the most impudent piece of brass that ever spoke with a tongue. He has taken possession of the easy-chair by the fireside already. He took off his boots in the parlor, and desired me to see them taken care of. (*quizzically*) I'm desirous to know how his impudence affects my daughter. (*shaking his head*) She will certainly be shocked at it.

Miss Hardcastle's entrance from the door at the left comes as a great surprise to the audience because the fashionably dressed young lady of the preceding scene has been replaced by a very pretty girl whose plain dress and little white apron make her easily mistaken for a chambermaid.

HARDCASTLE: (*surprised at her appearance and obviously pleased*) Well, my Kate, I see you have changed your dress, as I bid you; (*with considerable lack of comprehension at her docility on this particular occasion*) and yet, I believe, there was no great occasion.

MISS HARDCASTLE: (*primly*) I find such a pleasure, sir, in obeying your commands, that I take care to observe them without ever debating their propriety.

HARDCASTLE: (*very curious about her reaction to Marlow*) And yet, Kate, I *sometimes* give you *some* cause, particularly when I recommended my *modest* gentleman to you as a lover today.

MISS HARDCASTLE: (*in amused agreement*) You taught me to expect something extraordinary, and I find the original exceeds the description.

HARDCASTLE: (*interpreting "extraordinary" by his own experience with Marlow*) I was never so surprised in my life! He has quite confounded all my faculties!

MISS HARDCASTLE: (*in hearty agreement*) I never saw anything like it; and a man of the world, too!

HARDCASTLE: (*sententiously*) Ay, he learned it all abroad,—what a fool was I, to think a young man could learn modesty by traveling. (*snorting*) He might as well learn wit at a masquerade.

MISS HARDCASTLE: (*disagreeing*) It seems all natural to him.

HARDCASTLE: (*brusquely and disdainfully*) A good deal assisted by bad company and a French dancing master.

MISS HARDCASTLE: (*now completely baffled by her father's innuendoes*) Sure, you mistake, papa! A French dancing master could never have taught him that timid look—that awkward address—that bashful manner—

HARDCASTLE: (*interrupting with amazement*) Whose look, whose manner, child?

MISS HARDCASTLE: Mr. Marlow's: his *mauvaise honte,*[1] his timidity, struck me at the first sight.

HARDCASTLE: (*authoritatively*) Then your first sight deceived you; for I think him one of the most brazen first sights that ever astonished my senses.

MISS HARDCASTLE: (*puzzled*) Sure, sir, you rally! I never saw anyone so modest.

HARDCASTLE: (*raising his voice*) And can you be serious! I never saw such a bouncing swaggering puppy since I was born. Bully Dawson[2] was but a fool to him.

---

[1] Shame-faced appearance.

[2] An infamous scoundrel of a past generation.

MISS HARDCASTLE: (*protesting*) Surprising! He met me with a respectful bow, a stammering voice, and a look fixed on the ground.

HARDCASTLE: (*sharply*) He met *me* with a loud voice, a lordly air, and a familiarity that made my blood freeze again.

MISS HARDCASTLE: (*wonderingly*) He treated me with diffidence and respect; censured the manners of the age; admired the prudence of girls that never laughed; tired me with apologies for being tiresome; then left the room with a bow, and "Madam, I would not for the world detain you."

HARDCASTLE: (*enraged again at the memory*) He spoke to *me* as if he knew me all his life before. Asked twenty questions, and never waited for an answer. Interrupted my best remarks with some silly pun; and when I was in my best story of the Duke of Marlborough and Prince Eugene, he asked if I had not a good hand at making punch. (*as if unable to believe this final outrage himself*) Yes, Kate, he asked *your father* if he was a maker of punch!

MISS HARDCASTLE: (*at a loss*) One of us must certainly be mistaken.

HARDCASTLE: (*with parental firmness*) If he be what he has shown himself, I'm determined he shall never have my consent.

MISS HARDCASTLE: (*spiritedly*) And if he be the sullen thing *I* take him, he shall *never* have *mine*.

HARDCASTLE: (*pleased*) In one thing then we are agreed—to reject him.

MISS HARDCASTLE: (*in a hesitating voice of prudent temporizing, because of a new interest in Marlow prompted by her father's strange remarks*) Yes. But upon conditions. (*thoughtfully*) For if you should find him less impudent, and I more presuming; if you find him more respectful, and I more importunate—(*uncertainly*) —I don't know—the fellow is well enough for a man—

(*brightly advancing a point in his favor*) Certainly we don't meet many such at a horse race in the country.

HARDCASTLE: (*heavily*) If we should find him so— (*brushing off the absurd suggestion*) But that's impossible. The first appearance has done my business. I'm seldom deceived in that.

MISS HARDCASTLE: (*defensively*) And yet there may be many good qualities under that first appearance.

HARDCASTLE: (*with scornful condescension*) Ay, when a girl finds a fellow's *outside* to her taste, she then sets about guessing the rest of his furniture. With her, a smooth face stands for good sense, and a genteel figure for every virtue.

MISS HARDCASTLE: (*putting him on the defensive*) I hope, sir, a conversation begun with a compliment to my good sense won't end with a sneer at my understanding?

HARDCASTLE: (*apologetically*) Pardon me, Kate. (*indulging her whim*) But if young Mr. Brazen can find the art of reconciling contradictions, he may please us both, perhaps.

MISS HARDCASTLE: (*piqued by her curiosity*) And as one of us must be mistaken, what if we go to make further discoveries?

HARDCASTLE: Agreed. (*pontifically as he turns to go*) But depend on't, I'm in the right.

MISS HARDCASTLE: (*her eyes brightening in renewed interest in Marlow*) And, depend on't, I'm not *much* in the wrong. (*She gives his arm an affectionate squeeze as they go off to the left together.*)

A moment later, Tony comes running in from the right, clutching a casket.

TONY: (*exuberantly*) Ecod! I have got them. Here they are. My cousin Con's necklaces, bobs,[3] and all. My mother shan't cheat the poor souls out their fortune

---

[3] Pendants.

neither. (*startled suddenly at seeing Hastings enter from the door at the right*) O! my genius, is that you?

HASTINGS: (*in a low tone of secrecy befitting their private agreement*) My dear friend, how have you managed with your mother? I hope you have amused her with pretending love for your cousin, and that you are willing to be reconciled at last? Our horses will be refreshed in a short time, and we shall soon be ready to set off.

TONY: (*excitedly holding out the casket to him at arm's length and making no effort to subdue his voice*) And here's something to bear your charges by the way— (*Hastings takes the casket.*)—your sweetheart's jewels. Keep them, and hang those, I say, that would rob you of one of them.

HASTINGS: (*utterly amazed and somewhat disconcerted*) But how have you procured them from your mother?

TONY: (*glibly*) Ask me no questions, and I'll tell you no fibs. I procured them by the rule of thumb. If I had not a key to every drawer in my mother's bureau, how could I go to the alehouse so often as I do? An honest man may rob himself of his own at any time.

HASTINGS: (*agreeable to the results but a bit scrupulous about the timing*) Thousands do it every day. But, to be plain with you, Miss Neville is endeavoring to procure them from her aunt this very instant. If she succeeds, it will be the most delicate way, at least, of obtaining them. (*offering to give back the casket*)

TONY: (*with blatant realism*) Well, keep them, till you know how it will be. But I know how it will be well enough; she'd as soon part with the only sound tooth in her head.

HASTINGS: (*still extending the casket to him*) But I dread the effects of her resentment, when she finds she has lost them.

TONY: (*callously brushing him off*) Never you mind her resentment; leave *me* to manage that. I don't value her resentment the bounce of a cracker. (*suddenly aware of his mother and her niece about to enter from the left*) Zounds! here they are! (*pushing Hastings violently back out the right door*) Morrice![4] Prance!

Mrs. Hardcastle enters in the midst of an argument with her niece.

MRS. HARDCASTLE: (*in an outraged tone*) Indeed, Constance, you amaze me. Such a girl as you want jewels? It will be time enough for jewels, my dear, twenty years hence, when your beauty begins to want repairs.

MISS NEVILLE: (*insistently*) But what will repair beauty at forty will certainly improve it at twenty, madam.

MRS. HARDCASTLE: (*changing her tactics to indulgent flattery*) Yours, my dear can admit of none. That natural blush is beyond a thousand ornaments. (*in a worldly tone*) Besides, child, jewels are quite out at present. Don't you see half the ladies of our acquaintance, my Lady Kill-day-light, and Mrs. Crump, and the rest of them, carry their jewels to town, and bring nothing but paste and marcasites[5] back?

MISS NEVILLE: (*wheedling*) But who knows, madam, but somebody that shall be nameless would like me best with all my little finery about me?

MRS. HARDCASTLE: (*effusively*) Consult your glass, my dear, and then see, if with such a pair of eyes, you want any better sparklers. (*turning to Tony, insinuatingly*) What do you think, Tony, my dear? Does your cousin Con want any jewels, in your eyes, to set off her beauty?

TONY: (*noncommittally*) That's as thereafter may be.

MISS NEVILLE: (*pleading in her prettiest manner*) My *dear* aunt, if you knew how it would oblige me.

MRS. HARDCASTLE: (*deprecatingly*) A parcel of old-fashioned rose and table-cut[6] things. They would make

---

[4] The signal of a caller to begin a country dance.

[5] Crystallized forms of iron, an eighteenth century equivalent of costume jewelry.

[6] Methods of gem-cutting not used for the finest stones.

you look like the court of King Solomon at a puppet show. (*ruminatively*) Besides, I believe I can't readily come at them. They may be missing for aught I know to the contrary.

TONY: (*slyly, aside to his mother*) Then why don't you tell her so at once, as she's so longing for them? Tell her they're lost. It's the only way to quiet her. (*urgently*) Say they're lost, and call me to bear witness.

MRS. HARDCASTLE: (*aside to Tony*) You know, my dear, I'm only keeping them for you. (*her eyes lighting up as his suggestion begins to penetrate*) So if I say they're gone, you'll bear me witness, will you? (*with an idiotic titter as Tony nods agreement*) He! he! he!

TONY: (*aside to his mother*) Never fear me. Ecod! I'll say I saw them taken out with my own eyes.

MISS NEVILLE: (*not to be put off*) I desire them but for a day, madam; just to be permitted to show them as relics, and then they may be locked up again.

MRS. HARDCASTLE: (*as if forced to make an unpleasant revelation*) To be plain with you, my dear Constance, if I could find them you should have them. They're missing, I assure you. Lost, for aught I know; (*with gentle persuasiveness*) but we must have patience, wherever they are.

MISS NEVILLE: (*with irritation*) I'll not believe it; this is but a shallow pretense to deny me. I know they're too valuable to be so slightly kept, and as you are to answer for the loss—

MRS. HARDCASTLE: (*interrupting as if to calm a petulant child*) Don't be alarmed, Constance. If they be lost, I must restore an equivalent. But my son knows they are missing, and not to be found.

TONY: (*grinning solemnly*) That I can bear witness to. They are missing, and not to be found; I'll take my oath on't.

MRS. HARDCASTLE: (*sententiously*) You must learn resignation, my dear; for though we lose our fortune, yet we should not lose our patience. See me, how calm I am.

MISS NEVILLE: (*drily*) Ay, people are generally calm at the misfortunes of others.

MRS. HARDCASTLE: (*as if humoring a child*) Now, I wonder a girl of your good sense should waste a thought upon such trumpery. We shall soon find them; and, in the meantime, you shall make use of my garnets till your jewels be found.

MISS NEVILLE: (*flaring up bitterly*) I detest garnets.

MRS. HARDCASTLE: (*completely ignoring her outburst*) The most becoming things in the world to set off a clear complexion. You have often seen how well they look upon me. (*with settled determination as she sweeps out of the room through the door to left.*) You *shall* have them.

MISS NEVILLE: (*sulkily*) I dislike them of all things. (*sharply to Tony as he makes as if to follow his mother*) You shan't stir.—Was ever anything so provoking,—to mislay my own jewels, and force me to wear her trumpery?

TONY: (*speaking rapidly*) Don't be a fool. If she gives you the garnets, take what you can get. The jewels are your own already. I have stolen them out of her bureau, and she does not know it. (*nodding in the direction of the outer door to right*) Fly to your spark; he'll tell you more of the matter. Leave me to manage *her*.

MISS NEVILLE: (*overcome with delight*) My dear cousin!

TONY: (*urgently*) Vanish. She's here, and has missed them already. (*Miss Neville half runs, half dances off in the direction indicated. Tony directs his attention to the reentrance, opposite, of his mother.*) Zounds! how she fidgets and spits about like a Catherine wheel.[7]

MRS. HARDCASTLE: (*beside herself*) Confusion! thieves! robbers! we are cheated, plundered, broke open, undone!

---

[7] A revolving firework which shoots sparks in all directions.

TONY: (*as if with polite concern*) What's the matter, what's the matter, mamma? I hope nothing has happened to any of the good family?

MRS. HARDCASTLE: (*hysterical*) We are robbed. My bureau has been broke open, the jewels taken out, and I'm undone!

TONY: (*laughing as if greatly relieved*) Oh! is that all! Ha! ha! ha! By the laws, I never saw it better acted in my life. Ecod, I thought you was ruined in earnest, ha, ha, ha!

MRS. HARDCASTLE: (*with sober earnestness*) Why, boy, I *am* ruined in earnest. My bureau has been broken open, and all taken away.

TONY: (*noisily approving*) Stick to that; ha, ha, ha! stick to that. I'll bear witness, you know! call me to bear witness.

MRS. HARDCASTLE: (*close to tears of frustration*) I *tell* you, Tony, by all that's precious, the jewels are gone, and I shall be ruined forever.

TONY: (*with stolid loyalty*) Sure I know they're gone, and I am to say so.

MRS. HARDCASTLE: (*imploringly*) My *dearest* Tony, but hear me. They're *gone,* I say.

TONY: (*indulgently*) By the laws, mamma, you make me for to laugh, ha! ha! I know who took them well enough, ha! ha! ha!

MRS. HARDCASTLE: (*in tearful consternation*) Was there ever such a blockhead, that can't tell the difference between jest and earnest? I tell you I'm not in jest, booby.

TONY: (*nodding vigorously*) That's right, that's right! You must be in a bitter passion, and then nobody will suspect either of us. I'll bear witness that they are gone.

MRS. HARDCASTLE: (*almost screaming*) Was there *ever* such a cross-grained brute, that won't *hear* me! Can you bear witness that you're no better than a fool? Was *ever* poor woman so beset with fools on one hand, and thieves on the other?

TONY: (*nodding vigorously*) I can bear witness to that.

MRS. HARDCASTLE: (*raging*) Bear witness again, you blockhead you, and I'll turn you out of the room directly. (*with sudden anguish*) My poor niece, what will become of *her*? (*Tony guffaws.*) Do you *laugh,* you unfeeling brute, as if you *enjoyed* my distress?

TONY: (*nodding vigorously and increasingly enjoying the effect of the ritual repetition*) I can bear witness to that.

MRS. HARDCASTLE: (*raising her hand as if to strike him*) Do you insult me, monster? I'll teach you to vex your mother, I will!

TONY: (*with taunting defiance as he avoids her hand and edges off stage to right, still nodding vigorously*) I can bear witness to that. (*He breaks into a run; she follows him off stage in a wild fury.*)

Miss Hardcastle saunters in from the left, accompanied by a maid.

MISS HARDCASTLE: (*in a bemused tone*) What an unaccountable creature is that brother of mine, to send them to the house as an inn, ha! ha! I don't wonder at his impudence.

MAID: (*much amused but deferential*) But what is more, madam, the young gentleman, as you passed by in your present dress, asked me if you were the barmaid. (*as if stating the impossible*) He mistook you for the barmaid, madam.

MISS HARDCASTLE: (*her eyes twinkling roguishly*) Did he? Then as I live, I'm resolved to keep up the delusion. (*seriously*) Tell me, Pimple, how do you like my present dress? Don't you think I look something like Cherry[8] in the *Beaux' Stratagem*?

MAID: (*unwilling to agree that her mistress might look like a servant*) It's the dress, madam, that every lady wears in the country, but when she visits or receives company.

---

[8] The innkeeper's daughter in Farquhar's comedy.

MISS HARDCASTLE: (*intent on her scheme*) And are you sure he does not remember my face or person?

MAID: Certain of it.

MISS HARDCASTLE: (*musingly*) I vow I thought so; for though we spoke for some time together, yet his fears were such that he never once looked up during the interview. Indeed, if he had, my bonnet would have kept him from seeing me.

MAID: (*uncomprehending*) But what do you hope from keeping him in his mistake?

MISS HARDCASTLE: (*her face lighting in anticipation*) In the first place, I shall be *seen,* and that's no small advantage to a girl who brings her face to market. Then I shall perhaps make an acquaintance, and that's no small victory gained over one who never addresses any but the wildest of her sex. (*with forthright frankness*) But my chief aim is to take my gentleman off his guard, and like an invisible champion of romance examine the giant's force before I offer to combat.

MAID: (*tremulously*) But are you sure you can act your part, and disguise your voice so that he may mistake *that,* as he has already mistaken your person?

MISS HARDCASTLE: (*laughing*) Never fear me. I think I have got the true bar cant.[9] (*in a shrill voice*) Did your honor call?—Attend the Lion there.—Pipes and tobacco for the Angel.—The Lamb[10] has been outrageous this half hour.

MAID: (*with grudging admiration*) It will do, madam. (*in a sudden flurry as she sees Marlow about to enter from the left*) But he's here. (*She vanishes out the opposite door. Miss Hardcastle follows her and stands in the doorway as Marlow enters muttering angrily to himself.*)

MARLOW: What a bawling in every part of the house; I have scarce a moment's repose. If I go to the best room, there I find my host and his story. If I fly to the gallery,

---

[9] Barroom lingo.

[10] Lion, Angel, and Lamb would be the names of rooms in an inn, corresponding to room numbers in a modern hotel.

there we have my hostess with her curtsy down to the ground. I have at last got a moment to myself, and now for recollection.

He walks slowly up and down as if lost in thought. Miss Hardcastle watches him intently like a cat about to pounce. After a moment or two of this, she works her face into a brazen look and affects a coy and artless tone of voice which she maintains throughout her conversation with Marlow.

MISS HARDCASTLE: (*coming closer to him*) Did you call, sir? Did your honor call?

MARLOW: (*ignoring her existence and musing to himself*) As for Miss Hardcastle, she's too grave and sentimental for me.

MISS HARDCASTLE: (*advancing and placing herself directly in front of him*) Did your honor call?

MARLOW: (*off-handedly and turning away*) No, child. (*continuing his ruminations*) Besides, from the glimpse I had of her, I think she squints.

MISS HARDCASTLE: (*following him*) I'm sure, sir, I heard the bell ring.

MARLOW: (*with a trace of annoyance*) No, no. (*returning to his thoughts*) I have pleased my father, however, by coming down, and I'll tomorrow please myself by returning. (*He takes out his memorandum book and opens it as if to examine his future engagements.*)

MISS HARDCASTLE: (*insistently*) Perhaps the other gentleman called, sir?

MARLOW: (*sharply and without looking up*) I tell you no.

MISS HARDCASTLE: (*coming so close that he cannot avoid seeing her if he looks up*) I should be glad to know, sir. We have such a parcel of servants.

MARLOW: (*angrily*) No, no, I tell you. (*He looks her full in the face as he completes this determined dismissal, all but gasps in his sudden awareness of her fresh young beauty, and instantly changes his tone.*) Yes, child, I

think I did call. (*uncertainly*) I wanted—I wanted—
(*bursting out spontaneously*) I vow, child, you are *vastly*
handsome.

MISS HARDCASTLE: (*coyly, and stepping back a pace*)
O, la, sir, you'll make one ashamed.

MARLOW: (*now the confident young man about town*)
Never saw a more sprightly, malicious eye. Yes, yes, my
dear, I did call. Have you got any of your—a—what d'ye
call it in the house?

MISS HARDCASTLE: (*with another step backwards but
with no indication of not being used to handling flirtatious
customers*) No, sir, we have been out of that these ten
days.

MARLOW: (*closing the distance between them*) One
may call in this house, I find, to very little purpose. Suppose I should call for a taste, just by way of trial, of the
nectar of your lips; perhaps I might be disappointed in
that too.

MISS HARDCASTLE: (*pertly*) Nectar! nectar! That's a
liquor there's no call for in these parts. French, I suppose.
We keep no French wines here, sir.

MARLOW: (*with a frank appraisal of her figure*) Of
true English growth, I assure you.

MISS HARDCASTLE: (*retreating and pretending innocence*) Then it's odd I should not know it. We brew all
sorts of wines in this house, and I have lived here these
eighteen years.

MARLOW: (*genuinely surprised*) Eighteen years! Why,
one would think, child, you kept the bar before you were
born. How old *are* you?

MISS HARDCASTLE: (*demurely*) O! sir, I must not tell
my age. They say women and music should never be
dated.

MARLOW: (*scrutinizing her carefully*) To guess at this
distance, you can't be much above forty. (*moving closer
to her*) Yet nearer, I don't think so much. (*continuing
to close the distance between them*) By coming close to

some women, they look younger still; but when we come very close indeed— (*He attempts to kiss her, but she evades him by a quick movement and a light dance step away from him.*)

MISS HARDCASTLE: (*reprovingly*) Pray, sir, keep your distance. (*pertly*) One would think you wanted to know one's age as they do horses, by mark of mouth.

MARLOW: (*pouting*) I protest, child, you use me extremely ill. If you keep me at this distance, how is it possible you and I can ever be acquainted?

MISS HARDCASTLE: (*saucily*) And who wants to be acquainted with you? I want no such acquaintance, not I. I'm sure you did not treat Miss Hardcastle, that was here a while ago, in this obstropalous[11] manner. I'll warrant me, before her you looked dashed, and kept bowing to the ground, and talked, for all the world, as if you was before a justice of peace.

MARLOW: (*in a surprised aside*) Egad! she has hit it, sure enough. (*blusteringly, to her*) In awe of her, child? Ha! ha! ha! A mere awkward, squinting thing! No, no. I find you don't know me. I laughed, and rallied her a little; but I was unwilling to be too severe. No, I could not be too severe, *curse me!*

MISS HARDCASTLE: (*slyly*) O! then, sir, you are a favorite, I find, among the ladies?

MARLOW: (*exuding confidence*) Yes, my dear, a great favorite. And yet, hang me, I don't see what they find in me to follow. At the Ladies' Club in town, I'm called their agreeable Rattle. (*confidentially*) Rattle, child, is not my real name, but one I'm known by. (*with mock punctilio*) My name is Solomons. (*bowing*) Mr. Solomons, my dear, at your service. (*rises from his bow and steps forward to kiss her*)

MISS HARDCASTLE: (*interposing her hand*) Hold, sir;

---

[11] Her imitation of vulgarian lingo is particularly effective in this speech. She has probably overheard a servant using "obstropalous" for "obstreperous."

you are introducing me to your club, not to yourself. (*as if very much impressed*) And you're so great a favorite there, you say?

MARLOW: (*condescendingly*) Yes, my dear. There's Mrs. Mantrap, Lady Betty Blackleg, the Countess of Sligo, Mrs. Langhorns, old Miss Biddy Buckskin, and your humble servant keep up the spirit of the place.

MISS HARDCASTLE: (*meekly*) Then it's a very merry place, I suppose.

MARLOW: (*inflated by the impression he seems to be making*) Yes, as merry as cards, suppers, wine, and old women can make us.

MISS HARDCASTLE: (*with mocking laughter*) And their agreeable Rattle, ha! ha! ha!

MARLOW: (*a little deflated, to himself*) Egad! I don't quite like this chit. She looks knowing, methinks. (*to her, a trifle pompously*) You laugh, child?

MISS HARDCASTLE: (*with a gross pretense of simple-minded innocence*) I can't but laugh to think what time they all have for minding their work, or their family.

MARLOW: (*relieved, to himself*) All's well; she don't laugh at me. (*knowingly, to her*) Do *you* ever work, child?

MISS HARDCASTLE: (*again the simple-minded country servant-girl*) Ay, sure. There's not a screen or a quilt in the whole house but what can bear witness to *that*.

MARLOW: (*with kindly superiority*) Odso! then you must show me your embroidery. I embroider and draw patterns myself a little. If you want a judge of your work, you must apply to me. (*seizes her hand with great confidence just as Hardcastle enters from the left, takes in the scene, and halts abruptly in shocked surprise*)

MISS HARDCASTLE: Ay, but the colors don't look well by candlelight. You shall see all in the morning. (*struggling to release her hand*)

MARLOW: (*ardently*) And why not now, my angel? Such beauty fires beyond the power of resistance. (*Her*

*struggle pulls him around so that he suddenly becomes
aware of Hardcastle's presence. He releases her abruptly,
turns, and makes an unceremonious exit to the right as
he mutters angrily to himself in terms reminiscent of his
similar bad luck at dice.*) Pshaw! the father here! My old
luck; I never nicked seven that I did not throw ames ace
three times following.

HARDCASTLE: (*alone with his daughter, sarcastically*)
So. Madam! So I find *this* is your *modest* lover. This is
your humble admirer, that kept his eyes fixed on the
ground, and only adored at humble distance. (*reproachfully*) Kate, Kate, art thou not ashamed to deceive your
father so?

MISS HARDCASTLE: (*earnestly*) Never trust me, dear
papa, but he's still the modest man I first took him for;
you'll be convinced of it as well as I.

HARDCASTLE: (*outraged*) By the hand of my body, I
believe his impudence is infectious! Didn't I see him
seize your hand? Didn't I see him haul you about like a
milkmaid? And now you talk of his respect and his
modesty, forsooth!

MISS HARDCASTLE: (*with assurance that further be-
wilders the puzzled father*) But if I shortly convince you
of his modesty, that he has only the faults that will pass
off with time, and the virtues that will improve with age,
I hope you'll forgive him.

HARDCASTLE: (*shouting with consternation*) The girl
would actually make one run mad! I tell you I'll *not* be
convinced. (*pausing a moment reflectively and continuing with a somewhat quieter tone of authoritative determination*) I *am* convinced. He has scarcely been three
hours in the house, and he has already encroached on all
my prerogatives. *You* may like his impudence, and call it
modesty; but *my* son-in-law, madam, must have *very
different qualifications*.

MISS HARDCASTLE: (*mildly*) Sir, I ask but this night
to convince you.

HARDCASTLE: (*bluntly*) You shall not have half the time, for I have thoughts of turning him out this very hour.

MISS HARDCASTLE: (*with confidence*) Give me that hour, then, and I hope to satisfy you.

HARDCASTLE: (*with gruff indulgence*) Well, an hour let it be then. But I'll have no trifling with your father. All fair and open, do you mind me?

MISS HARDCASTLE: (*affectionately*) I hope, sir, you have ever found that I considered your commands as my pride; for your kindness is such, that my duty as yet has been inclination. (*He makes a slightly dubious grimace, but is obviously captivated by his daughter as they go off together to the left.*)

ACT FOUR

The same room, an hour later. Hastings and Miss Neville enter from the right engaged in earnest conversation.

HASTINGS: (*skeptically*) You surprise me! Sir Charles Marlow expected here this night? Where have you had your information?

MISS NEVILLE: (*insistently*) You may depend upon it. I just saw his letter to Mr. Hardcastle, in which he tells him he intends setting out a few hours after his son.

HASTINGS: (*disturbed*) Then, my Constance, all must be completed before he arrives. He knows me; and should he find me here, would discover my name, and perhaps my designs, to the rest of the family.

MISS NEVILLE: (*nervously*) The jewels, I hope, are safe.

HASTINGS: (*hastily*) Yes, yes. I have sent them to Marlow, who keeps the keys of our baggage. In the meantime, I'll go to prepare matters for our elopement. I have had the Squire's promise of a fresh pair of horses; and, if I should not see him again, will write him further directions. (*He blows her a kiss as he goes off through the door to right.*)

MISS NEVILLE: (*calling after him*) Well! success attend you. (*turning and thinking aloud as she walks off-stage to left*) In the meantime, I'll go amuse my aunt with the old pretense of a violent passion for my cousin.

Marlow enters from the right, followed by a servant.

116

MARLOW: (*bemused*) I wonder what Hastings could mean by sending me so valuable a thing as a casket to keep for him, when he knows the only place I have is the seat of a post coach at an inn door. (*directly to the servant*) Have you deposited the casket with the landlady, as I ordered you? Have you put it into her own hands?

SERVANT: Yes, your honor.

MARLOW: She said she'd keep it safe, did she?

SERVANT: (*emphatically*) Yes; she said she'd keep it safe enough; she asked me how I came by it; and she said she had a great mind to make me give an account of myself. (*He exits to the left.*)

MARLOW: (*amused by the effect of a jewel-casket on simple country people*) Ha! ha! ha! They're safe, however. (*wonderingly*) What an unaccountable set of beings have we got amongst! (*as if surprised at his own reactions*) This little barmaid, though, runs in my head most strangely, and drives out the absurdities of all the rest of the family. (*gazing toward the door to left*) She's mine, she must be mine, or I'm greatly mistaken. (*begins to walk about jubilantly on his toes*)

Hastings enters quickly from the right immersed in his urgent preparations for flight to such an extent that he is momentarily oblivious of Marlow. He stops abruptly as he is struck by a sudden thought.

HASTINGS: (*annoyed with himself*) Bless me! I quite forgot to tell her that I intended to prepare at the bottom of the garden. (*becoming aware of his friend*) Marlow here, and in spirits too.

MARLOW: (*seeing Hastings as he turns, in high spirits*) Give me joy, George! Crown me, *shadow* me with laurels! Well, George, after all, we modest fellows don't want for success among the women.

HASTINGS: (*sardonically*) Some women, you mean. But what success has your honor's modesty been crowned with now, that it grows so insolent upon us?

MARLOW: (*excitedly*) Didn't you see the tempting, brisk, lovely little thing, that runs about the house with a bunch of keys to its girdle?

HASTINGS: (*playing dumb*) Well! and what then?

MARLOW: (*rhapsodically*) She's mine, you rogue, you. Such fire, such motion, such eyes, such lips— (*realistically*) But, egad! she would not let me kiss them though.

HASTINGS: (*with playful skepticism, knowing Kate's real identity*) But are you so *sure,* so very *sure* of her?

MARLOW: (*crowing*) Why, man, she talked of showing me her work abovestairs, and I am to improve the pattern.

HASTINGS: (*pretending shock*) But how can *you,* Charles, go about to rob a woman of her honor?

MARLOW: (*easily*) Pshaw! pshaw! We all know the honor of the barmaid of an inn. I don't intend to *rob* her, take my word for it; there's nothing in this house I shan't honestly *pay* for.

HASTINGS: (*secretly highly amused*) I believe the girl has virtue.

MARLOW: (*agreeably but with a faint touch of priggery*) And if she has, I should be the last man in the world that would attempt to corrupt it.

HASTINGS: (*returning to his own affairs*) You have taken care, I hope, of the casket I sent you to lock up? It's in safety?

MARLOW: (*reassuringly*) Yes, yes. It's safe enough. I have taken care of it. But how could you think the seat of a post coach at an inn door a place of safety? Ah! numskull! I have taken better precautions for you than you did for yourself—I have—

HASTINGS: (*alarmed*) What?

MARLOW: (*with the quiet assurance of a superior in worldly matters*) I have sent it to the landlady to keep for you.

HASTINGS: (*aghast*) To the *landlady?*

MARLOW: (*blandly*) The landlady.

HASTINGS: (*in a daze*) You did?

MARLOW: (*offhandedly*) I did. She's to be answerable for its forthcoming, you know.

HASTINGS: (*miserably*) Yes, she'll bring it forth, —with a witness.

MARLOW: (*at a loss to understand his friend's peculiar reactions*) Wasn't I right? (*a bit huffily*) I believe you'll allow that I acted prudently upon this occasion?

HASTINGS: (*aside*) He must not see my uneasiness.

MARLOW: You seem a little disconcerted though, methinks. Sure nothing has happened?

HASTINGS: (*with forced casualness*) No, nothing. Never was in better spirits in all my life. And so you left it with the landlady, who, no doubt, very readily undertook the charge?

MARLOW: (*with amusement*) Rather too readily. For she not only kept the casket, but, through her great precaution, was going to keep the messenger too. Ha! ha! ha!

HASTINGS: (*with a hollow, half hysterical laugh*) He! he! he! They're *safe,* however.

MARLOW: (*radiating assurance*) As a guinea in a miser's purse.

HASTINGS: (*lugubriously to himself*) So now all hopes of fortune are at an end, and we must set off without it. (*to Marlow, with suppressed bitterness*) Well, Charles, I'll leave you to your meditations on the pretty barmaid, he! he! he! may you be as successful for yourself as you have been for me. (*He goes off rapidly to right.*)

MARLOW: (*looking after him*) Thank ye, George! I ask no more. Ha! ha! ha!

While Marlow continues to watch his friend's departure, Hardcastle enters from the left, muttering angrily.

HARDCASTLE: I no longer know my own house. It's turned all topsy-turvy. His servants have got drunk already. I'll bear it no longer; and yet from my respect for his father, I'll be calm. (*becoming conscious of Marlow's back across the stage*) Mr. Marlow, your servant. (*Mar-*

low turns around. Hardcastle continues with a low bow and exaggerated politeness.) I'm your very humble servant.

MARLOW: (*perfunctorily returning the bow*) Sir, your humble servant. (*aside*) What's to be the wonder now?

HARDCASTLE: (*stiffly*) I believe, sir, you must be sensible, sir, that no man alive ought to be more welcome than your father's son, sir. I hope you think so?

MARLOW: (*amusing himself at the expense of this old fool of an innkeeper*) I do from my soul, sir. I don't want much entreaty. I generally make my father's son welcome wherever he goes.

HARDCASTLE: (*caustically*) I believe you do, from my soul, sir. But though I say nothing to your own conduct, that of your servants is insufferable. Their manner of drinking is setting a very bad example in this house, I assure you.

MARLOW: (*seriously*) I protest, my very good sir, that's no fault of mine. If they don't drink as they ought, *they* are to blame. I ordered them not to spare the cellar. I did, I assure you. (*calling offstage to right*) Here, let one of my servants come up. (*to Hardcastle*) My positive directions were, that as I did not drink myself, they should make up for my deficiencies below.

HARDCASTLE: (*breathing heavily with suppressed outrage*) Then they had your orders for what they do! I'm satisfied!

MARLOW: (*with innocent aggressiveness and righteousness*) They had, I assure you. You shall hear from one of themselves.

A drunken servant comes reeling in at the right.

MARLOW: (*sharply*) You, Jeremy! Come forward, sirrah! What were my orders? Were you not told to drink freely, and call for what you thought fit, for the good of the house?

HARDCASTLE: (*aside, weak from emotion*) I begin to lose my patience.

JEREMY: Please you honor, liberty and Fleet Street forever![1] Though I'm but a servant, I'm as good as another man. I'll drink for no man before supper, sir, dammy! Good liquor will sit upon a good supper, but a good supper will not sit upon—hiccup—upon my conscience, sir. (*He all but falls.*)

MARLOW: (*agreeably as though clothed in a white garment of justification*) You see, my old friend, the fellow is as drunk as he can possibly be. I don't know what you'd have more, unless you'd have the poor devil soused in a beer barrel.

HARDCASTLE: (*aside, trembling with rage*) Zounds! he'll drive me distracted if I contain myself any longer. (*to Marlow, with cold precision*) Mr. Marlow, sir! I have submitted to your insolence for more than four hours, and I see no likelihood of its coming to an end. I'm now resolved to be master here, sir, and I desire that you and your drunken pack may leave my house directly.

MARLOW: (*uncomprehending and annoyed*) Leave your house! Sure you jest, my good friend? What? when I am doing what I can to please you!

HARDCASTLE: (*firmly with rising temperature*) I tell you, sir, you don't please me; so I desire you'll leave my house.

MARLOW: (*quizzically and half laughing*) Sure you cannot be serious? At this time o' night, and such a night. You only mean to banter me?

HARDCASTLE: (*raising his voice*) I tell you, sir, I'm serious; and now that my passions are roused, I say this house is mine, sir; this house is mine, and I command you to leave it directly.

MARLOW: (*quite undaunted and scarcely knowing what to make of this effrontery*) Ha! ha! ha! A puddle in a storm. I shan't stir a step, I assure you. (*evenly*) This is *your* house, fellow! It's *my* house. This is my house.

---

[1] The popular slogan of the political firebrand John Wilkes, considered a rabble-rouser by the upper classes.

Mine, while I choose to stay. (*raising his voice*) What right have you to bid me leave this house, sir? (*louder*) I never met with such impudence, curse me, never in my whole life before.

HARDCASTLE: (*outshouting him*) Nor I, confound me if ever I did! To come to my house, to call for what he likes, to turn me out of my own chair, to insult the family, to order his servants to get drunk, and then to tell me *This house is mine, sir!* (*breathing hard and resuming in a quieter tone*) By all that's impudent, it makes me laugh. Ha! ha! ha! (*with heavy sarcasm*) Pray, sir, as you take the house, what think you of taking the rest of the furniture? There's a pair of silver candlesticks, and there's a fire screen, and here's a pair of brazen-nosed bellows; perhaps you may take a fancy to them?

MARLOW: (*with icy civility*) Bring me your bill, sir, bring me your bill, and let's make no more words about it.

HARDCASTLE: (*so worked up that he scarcely hears him*) There are a set of prints, too. What think you of the *Rake's Progress*[2] for your own apartment?

MARLOW: (*angrily*) Bring me your bill, I say, and I'll leave you and your infernal house directly.

HARDCASTLE: (*continuing his tirade*) Then there's a mahogany table that you may see your own face in.

MARLOW: (*shouting*) My bill, I say.

HARDCASTLE: (*close to delirium*) I had forgot the great chair, for your own particular slumbers, after a hearty meal.

MARLOW: (*bellowing*) Zounds! bring me my bill, I say, and let's hear no more on't.

HARDCASTLE: (*breathing hard and forcing himself to control his voice*) Young man, young man, from your father's letter to me, I was taught to expect a well-bred, modest man as a visitor here, but now I find him no better than a coxcomb and a bully; but he will be down here

---

[2] A famous set of Hogarth engravings depicting the gradual degeneration of a young profligate.

presently, shall hear more of it. (*He turns abruptly and goes off to right.*)

MARLOW: (*bewildered and suddenly checked as though hit by an electric shock; to himself*) How's this! Sure I have not mistaken the house! Everything *looks* like an inn. The servants cry "coming." The attendance is awkward; the barmaid, too, to attend us. (*sees Miss Hardcastle about to enter from the left*) But she's here, and will inform me. (*Miss Hardcastle walks briskly in as if intending simply to pass through the room.*) Whither so fast, child? A word with you.

MISS HARDCASTLE: (*in her barmaid's voice*) Let it be short then. I'm in a hurry. (*aside*) I believe he begins to find out his mistake, but it's too soon quite to undeceive him.

MARLOW: (*intently as she pauses*) Pray, child, answer me one question. What are you, and what may your business in this house be?

MISS HARDCASTLE: (*laconically*) A relation of the family, sir.

MARLOW: (*probing*) What! a poor relation?

MISS HARDCASTLE: (*quickly picking up the cue for a new role*) Yes, sir, a poor relation, appointed to keep the keys, and to see that the guests want nothing in my power to give them.

MARLOW: (*encouragingly*) That is, you act as the barmaid of this inn.

MISS HARDCASTLE: (*joyously entertained*) Inn! O law —what brought that in your head? One of the best families in the county keep an inn! Ha! ha! ha! Old Mr. Hardcastle's house an inn!

MARLOW: (*reeling from the final shock of full comprehension*) Mr. Hardcastle's house! Is *this* house Mr. Hardcastle's house, child?

MISS HARDCASTLE: (*matter-of-factly*) Ay, sure. Whose else should it be?

MARLOW: (*visibly shaken*) So then all's out, and I

have been damnably imposed on. (*miserably*) O, confound my stupid head, I shall be laughed at over the whole town. I shall be stuck up in caricatura in all the print shops. The Dulissimo-Macaroni.[3] To mistake this house, of all others, for an inn, and my father's old friend for an innkeeper! What a swaggering puppy must he take me for! What a silly puppy do I find myself! (*ruefully, to her*) There, again, may I be hanged, my dear, but I mistook you for the barmaid.

MISS HARDCASTLE: (*with an affected simper*) Dear me! dear me! I'm sure there's nothing in my *behavior* to put me upon a level with one of that stamp.

MARLOW: (*humbly*) Nothing, my dear, nothing! But I was in for a list of blunders, and could not help making you a subscriber. My stupidity saw everything the wrong way. I mistook your assiduity for assurance, and your simplicity for allurement. (*tragically*) But it's over—this house I no more show *my* face in.

MISS HARDCASTLE: (*as if about to burst into tears*) I hope, sir, I have done nothing to disoblige you. I'm sure I should be sorry to affront any gentleman who has been so polite, and said so many civil things to me. (*sobbing*) I'm sure I should be sorry if he left the family upon my account. I'm sure I should be sorry people said anything amiss, since I have no fortune but my character.

MARLOW: (*aside*) By Heaven, she weeps. This is the first mark of tenderness I ever had from a modest woman, and it touches me. (*gently, to her*) Excuse me, my lovely girl, you are the only part of the family I leave with reluctance. (*but feeling obligated to point out the difference in their stations*) But to be plain with you, the difference of our birth, fortune, and education, make an

---

[3] Eighteenth century caricaturists sold candid portraits of celebrities, revealing them in typical or sometimes unguarded moments in their lives. Marlow suggests an appropriate title, meaning the "dullest young dandy," for the one certain to be drawn to depict him in his present embarrassment.

honorable connection impossible and I can never harbor a thought of seducing simplicity that trusted in my honor, or bringing ruin upon one whose only fault was being too lovely.

MISS HARDCASTLE: (*aside*) Generous man. I now begin to admire him. (*reassuming her role, to him*) But I'm sure my family is as good as Miss Hardcastle's, and though I'm poor, that's no great misfortune to a contented mind; and, until this moment, I never thought that it was bad to want[4] fortune.

MARLOW: (*pretending not to understand*) And why now, my pretty simplicity?

MISS HARDCASTLE: (*with child-like candor*) Because it puts me at a distance from one, that if I had a thousand pound I would give it all to.

MARLOW: (*aside*) This simplicity bewitches me so, that if I stay I'm undone. I must make one bold effort and leave her. (*solemnly, to her*) Your partiality in my favor, my dear, touches me most sensibly; and were I to live for myself alone, I could easily fix my choice. But I owe too much to the opinion of the world, too much to the authority of a father, (*choking with emotion*) so that —I can scarcely speak it—it affects me. Farewell. (*He turns with determination and exits to right.*)

MISS HARDCASTLE: (*musing aloud*) I never knew half his merit till now. He shall not go, if I have power or art to detain him. I'll still preserve the character in which I stooped to conquer, but will undeceive my papa, who, perhaps, may laugh him out of his resolution. (*She goes off pensively to the left.*)

Tony and Miss Neville enter from the right, engaged in earnest conversation.

TONY: (*sullenly*) Ay, you may steal for yourselves the next time. I have done my duty. She has got the jewels again, that's a sure thing; but she believes it was all a mistake of the servants.

---

[4] To be in want of.

MISS NEVILLE: (*pleadingly*) But, my dear cousin, sure you won't forsake us in this distress? If she in the least suspects that I am going off, I shall certainly be locked up, or sent to my aunt Pedigree's, which is ten times worse.

TONY: (*agreeably*) To be sure, aunts of all kinds are damned bad things. But what can I do? I have got you a pair of horses that will fly like Whistle Jacket,[5] and I'm sure you can't say but I have courted you nicely before her face. (*pulling her backstage as he catches sight of his mother about to enter from the left*) Here she comes. We must court a bit or two more, for fear she should suspect us.

They embrace and pretend to be whispering sweet nothings as Mrs. Hardcastle enters.

MRS. HARDCASTLE: (*talking to herself*) Well, I was greatly fluttered, to be sure. But my son tells me it was all a mistake of the servants. (*shaking her head*) I shan't be easy, however, till they are fairly married, and then let her keep her own fortune. (*espying the lovers*) But what do I see! Fondling together, as I'm alive. I never saw Tony so sprightly before. (*calling fatuously to them*) Ah! have I caught you, my pretty doves! What, billing, exchanging stolen glances, and broken murmurs! (*rapturously*) Ah!

TONY: (*true to his role*) As for murmurs, mother, we grumble a little now and then, to be sure. But there's no love *lost* between us.

MRS. HARDCASTLE: (*cooing*) A mere sprinkling, Tony, upon the flame, only to make it burn brighter.

MISS NEVILLE: (*in a syrupy voice*) Cousin Tony promises to give us more of his company at home. Indeed, he shan't leave us any more. (*in baby-talk*) It won't leave us, Cousin Tony, will it?

TONY: (*close to nausea but with determined gallantry*) O! it's a pretty creature. No, I'd sooner leave my horse in

---

[5] A champion race-horse.

a pound, than leave you when you smile upon one so. Your laugh makes you so becoming.

MISS NEVILLE: (*rapturously*) Agreeable cousin! Who can help admiring that natural humor, that pleasant, broad, red, thoughtless (*patting his cheek rather harder than necessary*), —ah! it's a bold face.

MRS. HARDCASTLE: (*beaming idiotically*) Pretty innocence.

TONY: (*keeping up his end with the greatest of difficulty*) I'm sure I always loved cousin Con's hazel eyes, and her pretty long fingers, that she twists this way and that over the haspicholls, like a parcel of bobbins.[6]

MRS. HARDCASTLE: (*overcome with joy*) Ah, he would charm the bird from the tree. I was never so happy before. My boy takes after his father, poor Mr. Lumpkin, exactly. The jewels, my dear Con, shall be yours incontinently. You shall have them. (*cooing*) Isn't he a sweet boy, my dear? You shall be married tomorrow, and we'll put off the rest of his education, like Dr. Drowsy's sermons, to a fitter opportunity.

DIGGORY: (*entering from the right door with a letter in his hand*) Where's the Squire? (*seeing him*) I have got a letter for your worship.

TONY: (*unable to read*) Give it to my mamma. She reads all my letters first.

DIGGORY: I had orders to deliver it into your own hands.

TONY: Who does it come from?

DIGGORY: (*noncommittally*) Your worship mun ask that o' the letter itself. (*He thrusts the letter at Tony and leaves.*)

TONY: (*examining the letter while turning it over and over*) I could wish to know, though.

MISS NEVILLE: (*aside*) Undone, undone. A letter to

---

[6] Her fingers in playing the harpsichord are compared to the bobbins shuttling back and forth to provide the cross threads in the manufacture of lace or other fabrics.

him from Hastings. I know the hand. If my aunt sees it, we are ruined forever. I'll keep her employed a little if I can. (*with forced gaiety to Mrs. Hardcastle*) But I have not told you, madam, of my cousin's smart answer just now to Mr. Marlow. We so laughed—you must know, madam—(*pulling her off to the side*)—this way a little, for he must not hear us. (*She whispers to her aunt while desperately signalling to Tony who stupidly ignores her.*)

TONY: (*dully gazing at the letter*) A damned cramp piece of penmanship, as ever I saw in my life. I can read your print-hand very well. But here there are such handles, and shanks, and dashes, that one can scarce tell the head from the tail. *To Anthony Lumpkin, Esquire.* It's very odd, I can read the outside of my letters, where my own name is, well enough. But when I come to open it, it's all—buzz. That's hard, very hard; for the inside of the letter is always the cream of the correspondence.

MRS. HARDCASTLE: (*much taken with the account of her son's cleverness*) Ha! ha! ha! Very well. Very well. And so my son was too hard for the philosopher.

MISS NEVILLE: (*secretively*) Yes, madam; but you must hear the rest, madam. A little more this way, or he may hear us. You'll hear how he puzzled him again. (*frowning and shaking her head at Tony*)

MRS. HARDCASTLE: (*glancing at Tony who is still puzzling over the letter*) He seems strangely puzzled now himself, methinks.

TONY: (*now attempting to decipher the letter itself*) A damned up-and-down hand, as if it was disguised in liquor. (*reading*) *Dear Sir,* (*sighing as if exhausted by the effort*) —Ay, that's that. Then there's an *M*, and a *T*, and an *S,* but whether the next be an *izzard*[7] or an *R,* confound me, I cannot tell.

MRS. HARDCASTLE: (*indulgently to Tony*) What's that, my dear; can I give you any assistance? (*Tony hands her the letter.*)

---

[7] Colloquial term for the letter *Z*.

MISS NEVILLE: (*with celerity*) Pray, aunt, let me read it. Nobody reads a cramp hand better than I. (*twitching the letter from her; addressing Tony*) Do you know who it is from?

TONY: Can't tell, except from Dick Ginger the feeder.

MISS NEVILLE: (*immensely relieved*) Ay, so it is. (*pretending to read*) Dear Squire, Hoping that you're in health, as I am at this present. The gentlemen of the Shake-bag club has cut the gentlemen of Goose-green quite out of feather. The odds—um—odd battle—um— long fighting—um—here, here—(*crumpling the letter and thrusting it at him*) It's all about cocks, and fighting; it's of no consequence. Here, put it up, put it up.

TONY: (*impetuously seizing the letter*) But I tell you, miss, it's of all the consequence in the world. I would not lose the rest of it for a guinea. Here, mother, *do* make it out. Of no consequence! (*giving Mrs. Hardcastle the letter*)

MRS. HARDCASTLE: (*peering at it*) How's this? (*reading*) Dear Squire, I'm now waiting for Miss Neville with a post chaise and pair, at the bottom of the garden, but I find my horses yet unable to perform the journey. I expect you'll assist us with a pair of fresh horses, as you promised. Dispatch is necessary as the HAG—ay, the hag— your mother, will otherwise suspect us. Yours, Hastings. (*exploding*) Grant me patience. I shall run distracted! My rage chokes me!

MISS NEVILLE: (*temporizing*) I hope, madam, you'll suspend your resentment for a few moments, and not impute to me any impertinence, or sinister design that belongs to another.

MRS. HARDCASTLE: (*curtsying very low*) Fine spoken, madam; you are most miraculously polite and engaging, and quite the very pink of courtesy and circumspection, madam. (*changing her tone to extreme bitterness as she turns to Tony*) And you, you great ill-fashioned oaf, with scarce sense enough to keep your mouth shut—were you too joined against me? (*to both of them*) But I'll defeat all your plots in a moment. (*to Miss Neville*) As for you, madam, since you have got a pair of fresh horses ready, it would be cruel to disappoint them. So, if you please, instead of running away with your spark, prepare, this very moment, to run off with *me*. Your old aunt Pedigree will keep you secure, I'll warrant me. (*to Tony*) You too, sir, may mount your horse, and guard us upon the way. (*calling*) Here, Thomas, Roger, Diggory! I'll show you that I wish you better than you do yourselves. (*She sweeps off to left.*)

MISS NEVILLE: (*tragically*) So now I'm completely ruined.

TONY: (*morosely*) Ay, that's a sure thing.

MISS NEVILLE: (*bitterly*) What better could be expected from being connected with such a stupid fool, and after all the nods and signs I made him!

TONY: (*defensively*) By the laws, miss, it was your own cleverness, and not my stupidity, that did your business. You were so nice and so busy with your Shakebags and Goose-greens that I thought you could never be making believe.

Hastings rushes in from the right door.

HASTINGS: (*accusingly to Tony*) So, sir, I find by my servant that you have shown my letter, and betrayed us. Was this well done, young gentleman?

TONY: (*sullenly*) Here's another. Ask miss there who betrayed you. Ecod, it was her doing, not mine.

Marlow enters from the right.

MARLOW: (*in high dudgeon*) So I have been finely used here among you. Rendered contemptible, driven into ill manners, despised, insulted, laughed at.

TONY: (*sulkily*) Here's another. We shall have old Bedlam[8] broke loose presently.

MISS NEVILLE: (*to Marlow*) And there, sir, (*pointing

---

[8] The common name for the insane asylum in London, Hospital of St. Mary of Bethlehem.

at Tony) is the gentleman to whom we all owe every obligation.

MARLOW: (*helplessly—in angry declamation*) What can I say to him? A mere boy, an idiot, whose ignorance and age are a protection.

HASTINGS: (*vehemently*) A poor contemptible booby, that would but disgrace correction.

MISS NEVILLE: (*with acidity*) Yet with cunning and malice enough to make himself merry with all our embarrassments.

HASTINGS: (*with cold fury*) An insensible cub.

MARLOW: (*in the same tone*) Replete with tricks and mischief.

TONY: (*exploding*) Baw! damme, but I'll fight you both, one after the other—with baskets.[9]

MARLOW: (*angrily, to Hastings*) As for him, he's below resentment. But your conduct, Mr. Hastings, requires an explanation. You knew of my mistakes, yet would not undeceive me.

HASTINGS: (*miserably*) Tortured as I am with my own disappointments, is this a time for explanations? It is not friendly, Mr. Marlow.

MARLOW: (*expostulating*) But, sir—

MISS NEVILLE: (*interrupting*) Mr. Marlow, we never kept on your mistake, till it was too late to undeceive you. Be pacified.

A maid enters from the left.

MAID: My mistress desires you'll get ready immediately, madam. The horses are putting to.[10] Your hat and things are in the next room. We are to go thirty miles before morning. (*The maid drops a perfunctory curtsey and retires.*)

MISS NEVILLE: (*fatalistically*) Well, well; I'll come presently.

---

[9] Duelling foils with basket-like hilts to protect the hand.
[10] Being harnessed to the chaise.

MARLOW: (*still clinging to his own discomfiture, to Hastings*) Was it well done, sir, to assist in rendering me ridiculous? To hang me out for the scorn of all my acquaintance? Depend upon it, sir, I shall expect an explanation.

HASTINGS: (*with equal spleen*) Was it well done, sir, if you're upon that subject, to deliver what I intrusted to yourself to the care of another, sir?

MISS NEVILLE: (*desolately*) Mr. Hastings. Mr. Marlow. Why will you increase my distress by this groundless dispute? I implore, I entreat you—

The maid reenters with a cloak.

MAID: Your cloak, madam. My mistress is impatient.

MISS NEVILLE: (*wearily taking the cloak*) I come. (*The maid leaves. Miss Neville turns imploringly to the two men.*) Pray, be pacified. If I leave you thus, I shall die with apprehension.

The maid comes in again with needed accessories which she thrusts at Miss Neville.

MAID: Your fan, muff, and gloves, madam. The horses are waiting. (*She retires again.*)

MISS NEVILLE: (*beseechingly, to Marlow*) O, Mr. Marlow! if you knew what a scene of constraint and ill nature lies before me, I'm sure it would convert your resentment into pity.

MARLOW: (*in a state of confusion*) I'm so distracted with a variety of passions, that I don't know what I do. (*recovering himself*) Forgive me, madam. George, forgive me. You know my hasty temper, and should not exasperate it.

HASTINGS: (*morosely*) The torture of my situation is my only excuse.

MISS NEVILLE: (*encouragingly, to Hastings*) Well, my dear Hastings, if you have that esteem for me that I think, that I am *sure* you have, your constancy for three years will but increase the happiness of our future connection. If—

MRS. HARDCASTLE: (*calling peremptorily from the adjoining room to the right.*) Miss Neville! Constance, why, Constance, I say!

MISS NEVILLE: (*dully*) I'm coming. (*tearfully, to Hastings*) Well, constancy. Remember, constancy is the word. (*With a last ardent gaze of farewell, she turns and goes off to the right with lowered head.*)

HASTINGS: (*in anguish*) My heart! how can I support this! To be so near happiness, and such happiness!

MARLOW: (*to Tony, who has been lost in a reverie during the preceding interchange*) You see now, young gentleman, the effects of your folly. What might be amusement to you is here disappointment, and even distress.

TONY: (*looking up smartly and as if not having heard Marlow's reproof*) Ecod, I have hit it. (*exultantly*) It's here. Your hands. (*to Marlow and then to Hastings*) Yours, and yours, my poor Sulky. (*seizes their hands and calls to right*) My boots there, ho! (*to the bewildered men*) Meet me two hours hence at the bottom of the garden; and if you don't find Tony Lumpkin a more good-natured fellow than you thought for, I'll give you leave to take my best horse, and Bet Bouncer into the bargain. (*pulling them out to right after him*) Come along. My boots, ho! (*They go off.*)

ACT FIVE

SCENE ONE

The same room some two hours later. Hastings enters from the right accompanied by one of his personal servants.

HASTINGS: You saw the old lady and Miss Neville drive off, you say?

SERVANT: Yes, your honor. They went off in a post coach, and the young Squire went on horseback. They're thirty miles off by this time.

HASTINGS: (*gloomily*) Then all my hopes are over.

SERVANT: (*noncommittally*) Yes, sir. Old Sir Charles is arrived. He and the old gentleman of the house have been laughing at Mr. Marlow's mistake this half hour. (*looking toward the left*) They are coming this way. (*He goes off to right.*)

HASTINGS: Then I must not be seen. So now to my fruitless appointment at the bottom of the garden. (*following the servant out*) This is about the time.

Hardcastle, laughing heartily, ushers in Sir Charles Marlow from the left. Sir Charles is obviously a city gentleman, soberly dressed as becomes his reserved disposition. The unobtrusiveness of his genteel bearing is in striking contrast to the effusive camaraderie of his countrified host.

HARDCASTLE: (*guffawing*) Ha! ha! ha! (*slapping his*

thigh) The peremptory tone in which he sent forth his sublime commands!

SIR CHARLES: (*ironically*) And the reserve with which I suppose he treated all your advances.

HARDCASTLE: (*his amusement suddenly giving way to pique*) And yet he might have seen something in me above a common innkeeper, too.

SIR CHARLES: (*his turn to be amused*) Yes, Dick, but he mistook you for an uncommon innkeeper, ha! ha! ha!

HARDCASTLE: (*amiably*) Well, I'm in too good spirits to think of anything but joy. Yes, my dear friend, this union of our families will make our personal friendships hereditary; and though my daughter's fortune is but small—

SIR CHARLES: (*dismissing such sordid details*) Why, Dick, will you talk of fortune to *me*? My son is possessed of more than a competence already, and can want nothing but a good and virtuous girl to share his happiness and increase it. If they like each other, as you say they do—

HARDCASTLE: (*explosively*) If, man! I tell you they *do* like each other. My daughter as good as told me so.

SIR CHARLES: (*realistically*) But girls are apt to flatter themselves, you know.

HARDCASTLE: (*with vehemence*) I saw him grasp her hand in the warmest manner myself; (*looking up to the right*) and here he comes to put you out of your *ifs*, I warrant him.

Marlow enters, obviously downcast, but with quiet dignity.

MARLOW: (*to Hardcastle, with decent humility*) I come, sir, once more, to ask pardon for my strange conduct. I can scarce reflect on my insolence without confusion.

HARDCASTLE: (*heartily*) Tut, boy, a trifle. You take it too gravely. An hour or two's laughing with my daughter will set all to rights again. She'll never like you the worse for it.

MARLOW: (*politely*) Sir, I shall be always proud of her approbation.

HARDCASTLE: (*insinuatingly*) Approbation is but a cold word, Mr. Marlow; if I am not deceived, you have something more than approbation thereabouts. You take me.[1]

MARLOW: (*disconcerted*) Really, sir, I have not that happiness.

HARDCASTLE: (*rallying him*) Come, boy, I'm an old fellow, and know what's what, as well as you that are younger. I know what has passed between you; (*conspiratorially placing his finger to his lips*) but mum. (*leering knowingly at him*)

MARLOW: (*in confusion*) Sure, sir, nothing has passed between us but the most profound respect on my side, and the most distant reserve on hers. You don't think, sir, that my impudence has been passed upon all the rest of the family?

HARDCASTLE: (*relishing the scene he has observed between Marlow and his daughter*) Impudence! No, I don't say that—not quite impudence—though girls like to be played with, and rumpled a little too sometimes. (*with a sly wink*) But she has told no tales, I assure you.

MARLOW: (*defensively*) I never gave her the slightest cause.

HARDCASTLE: (*annoyed at his hypocrisy*) Well, well, I like modesty in its place well enough. But this is over-acting, young gentleman. You *may* be open. Your father and I will like you the better for it.

MARLOW: (*protesting*) May I die, sir, if I ever—

HARDCASTLE: (*noisily overriding him*) I tell you she don't dislike you; and as I am sure you like her—

MARLOW: (*weakly*) Dear sir,—I protest, sir—

HARDCASTLE: (*ignoring him*) I see no reason why you should not be joined as fast as the parson can tie you.

---

[1] You follow me.

MARLOW: (*with more vigor*) But hear me, sir—

HARDCASTLE: (*settling everything*) Your father approves the match, I admire it, every moment's delay will be doing mischief, so—

MARLOW: (*interrupting with determination*) But why won't you hear me? By all that's just and true, I never gave Miss Hardcastle the slightest mark of my attachment, or even the most distant hint to suspect me of affection. We had but one interview, and that was formal, modest, and uninteresting.

HARDCASTLE: (*aside, gasping*) This fellow's formal, modest impudence is beyond bearing.

SIR CHARLES: (*intently*) And you never grasped her hand, or made any protestations?

MARLOW: (*firmly but quietly*) As heaven is my witness, I came down in obedience to your commands. I saw the lady without emotion, and parted without reluctance. I hope you'll exact no further proofs of my duty, nor prevent me from leaving a house in which I suffer so many mortifications. (*He bows stiffly and goes off to right.*)

SIR CHARLES: (*wonderingly*) I'm astonished at the air of sincerity with which he parted.

HARDCASTLE: (*indignantly*) And *I'm* astonished at the deliberate intrepidity of his assurance.

SIR CHARLES: (*soberly*) I dare pledge my life and honor upon his truth.

HARDCASTLE: (*looking to the left*) Here comes my daughter, and I would stake my happiness upon *her* veracity. (*Miss Hardcastle enters.*) Kate, come hither, child. Answer us sincerely and without reserve; has Mr. Marlow made you any profession of love and affection?

MISS HARDCASTLE: (*her color heightening*) The question is very abrupt, sir! But since you require unreserved sincerity, I think he has.

HARDCASTLE: (*to Sir Charles*) You see.

SIR CHARLES: (*his brow furrowing with perplexity*)

And pray, madam, have you and my son had more than one interview?

MISS HARDCASTLE: (*primly*) Yes, sir, several.

HARDCASTLE: (*triumphantly, to Sir Charles*) You see.

SIR CHARLES: (*painfully*) But did he profess any attachment?

MISS HARDCASTLE: (*with modest reserve*) A lasting one.

SIR CHARLES: (*as if unable to credit his ears*) Did he talk of love?

MISS HARDCASTLE: (*lowering her eyes*) Much, sir.

SIR CHARLES: (*shocked and dismayed*) Amazing! And all this formally?

MISS HARDCASTLE: (*looking up and addressing him with clear-cut finality*) Formally.

HARDCASTLE: (*grumpily*) Now, my friend, I hope you are satisfied.

SIR CHARLES: (*still skeptical, to Miss Hardcastle*) And *how* did he behave, madam?

MISS HARDCASTLE: (*off-handedly in parody of the formal stage-lover*) As most professed admirers do. Said some civil things of my face, talked much of his want of merit, and the greatness of mine; mentioned his heart, gave a short tragedy speech, and ended with pretended rapture.

SIR CHARLES: (*evincing enormous relief*) Now I'm perfectly convinced, indeed. I know his conversation among women to be modest and submissive. This forward, canting, ranting manner by no means describes him, and, I am confident, he never sat for the picture.

MISS HARDCASTLE: (*amiably ignoring the insult*) Then what, sir, if I should convince you to your face of my sincerity? If you and my papa, in about half an hour, will place yourselves behind that screen, you shall hear him declare his passion to me in person.

SIR CHARLES: Agreed. (*heavily*) And if I find him

what you describe, all my happiness in him must have an end. (*He goes off to left, brooding.*)

MISS HARDCASTLE: (*looking after him*) And if you don't find him what I describe—(*with a quizzical glance at her father*) I fear *my* happiness must never have a beginning. (*She goes off to the right, followed by her father.*)

Scene Two

The back of the garden, immediately following. A high clipped hedge backing up a formal garden is painted on the backdrop. Flowering bushes are suggested on the wings. Hastings wanders on from the right, muttering to himself in a sultry mood.

HASTINGS: What an idiot am I to wait here for a fellow, who probably takes a delight in mortifying me. He never intended to be punctual, and I'll wait no longer. (*perceiving someone moving toward him from the opposite side*) What do I see? It is he, and perhaps with news of my Constance. (*Tony, staggering from weariness, enters, booted and splattered*) My honest Squire! I now find you a man of your word. This looks like friendship.

TONY: (*in a tired and querulous voice*) Ay, I'm your friend, and the best friend you have in the world, if you knew but all. This riding by night, by the bye, is cursedly tiresome. It has shook me worse than the basket of a stagecoach.

HASTINGS: (*beside himself with curiosity*) But how? where did you leave your fellow travellers? Are they in safety? Are they housed?

TONY: (*mumbling*) Five and twenty miles in two hours and a half is no such bad driving. The poor beasts have smoked for it: rabbit me, but I'd rather ride forty miles after a fox than ten with such *varment*.

HASTINGS: (*urgently*) Well, but where have you left the ladies? I die with impatience.

TONY: (*dumbly*) Left them? Why, where should I leave them but where I found them?

HASTINGS: (*annoyed*) This is a riddle.

TONY: (*idiotically*) Riddle me this then. What's that goes round the house, and round the house, and never touches the house?

HASTINGS: (*disgusted but unwilling to offend his only possible friend*) I'm still astray.

TONY: (*very much pleased with himself*) Why, that's it, mon. I have led them astray. By jingo, there's not a pond or slough within five miles of the place but they can tell the taste of.

HASTINGS: (*with delighted comprehension*) Ha! ha! ha! I understand; you took them in a round, while they supposed themselves going forward. And so you have at last brought them home again.

TONY: (*swaggering*) You shall hear. I first took them down Feather-bed Lane, where we stuck fast in the mud. I then rattled them crack over the stones of Up-and-down Hill—I then introduced them to the gibbet on Heavy-tree Heath; and from that, with a circumbendibus,[1] I fairly lodged them in the horsepond at the bottom of the garden.

HASTINGS: (*fearfully*) But no accident, I hope.

TONY: (*reassuringly*) No, no. (*snickering*) Only mother is confoundedly frightened. She thinks herself forty miles off. She's sick of the journey, and the cattle can scarce crawl. So if your own horses be ready, you may whip off with Cousin, and I'll be bound that no soul here can budge a foot to follow you.

HASTINGS: (*overwhelmed with joyous anticipation*) My dear friend, how can I be grateful?

TONY: (*contentiously*) Ay, now it's *dear* friend, *noble* Squire. Just now, it was all idiot, cub, and run me through the guts. Damn *your* way of fighting, I say. After we take a knock in *this* part of the country, we kiss

---

[1] Tony's own term for a circuitous route.

and be friends. But if you had run me through the guts,
then I should be dead, and you might go kiss the hang-
man.

HASTINGS: (*humbly*) The rebuke is just. (*eagerly*) But
I must hasten to relieve Miss Neville; if you keep the old
lady employed, I promise to take care of the young one.

TONY: (*peering out to left*) Never fear me. Here she
comes. Vanish. (*Hastings dashes to rear and left*) She's
got from the pond, and draggled up to the waist like a
mermaid.

*Mrs. Hardcastle comes limping in, completely di-
sheveled and with her skirt soggy with muck.*

MRS. HARDCASTLE: (*hoarse and breathing hard*) Oh,
Tony, I'm killed. Shook! Battered to death! I shall never
survive it. That last jolt that laid us against the quickset
hedge has done by business.

TONY: (*unfeelingly*) Alack, mamma, it was all your
own fault. You *would* be for running away by night,
without knowing one inch of the way.

MRS. HARDCASTLE: (*weakly*) I wish we were at home
again. I never met so many accidents in so short a journey. Drenched in the mud, overturned in a ditch, stuck
fast in a slough, jolted to a jelly, and at last to lose our
way! (*pitiably*) Whereabouts do you think we are, Tony?

TONY: (*thoughtfully*) By my guess, we should be upon
Crack-skull Common, about forty miles from home.

MRS. HARDCASTLE: (*quivering with fatigue and fear*)
O lud! O lud! The most notorious spot in all the country.
We only want a robbery to make a complete night on't.

TONY: (*outrageously*) Don't be afraid, mamma, don't
be afraid. Two of the five that kept here are hanged, and
the other three may not find us. Don't be afraid. (*peering over her shoulder*) Is that a man that's galloping behind us? No, it's only a tree. Don't be afraid.

MRS. HARDCASTLE: (*gulping*) The fright will certainly
kill me.

TONY: (*pointing toward a bush on the right*) Do you

see anything like a black hat moving behind the thicket?

MRS. HARDCASTLE: (*gasping*) O death!

TONY: (*cheerfully*) No, it's only a cow. Don't be afraid, mamma, don't be afraid.

MRS. HARDCASTLE: (*in a suppressed scream*) As I'm alive, Tony, I see a man coming towards us. (*gulping*) Ah, I'm sure on't. (*wilting*) If he perceives us we are undone.

TONY: (*aside*) Father-in-law,[2] by all that's unlucky, come to take one of his night walks. (*frighteningly, to her*) Ah, it's a highwayman, with pistols as long as my arm. A damned ill-looking fellow.

MRS. HARDCASTLE: (*as if about to collapse*) Good heaven defend us! He approaches.

TONY: (*with urgency*) Do you hide yourself in that thicket (*pointing to bushes at the left*), and leave me to manage him. If there be any danger, I'll cough and cry hem. When I cough, be sure to keep close. (*Mrs. Hardcastle scurries behind the bushes.*)

HARDCASTLE: (*entering from the right and musing aloud*) I'm mistaken, or I heard voices of people in want of help. (*almost walking into Tony*) Oh, Tony, is that you? I did not expect you so soon back. Are your mother and her charge in safety?

TONY: (*dutifully*) Very safe, sir, at my aunt Pedigree's. (*noisily*) Hem.

MRS. HARDCASTLE: (*tremulously from behind the bushes*) Ah, death! I find there's danger.

HARDCASTLE: (*with paternal concern*) Forty miles in three hours; sure, that's too much, my youngster.

TONY: (*sententiously*) Stout horses and willing minds make short journeys, as they say. (*loudly*) Hem.

MRS. HARDCASTLE: (*from behind the bushes, sobbing*) Sure he'll do the dear boy no harm.

HARDCASTLE: (*peering uncertainly in the direction of*

---

2 Stepfather.

O lud! he'll murder my poor boy, my darling.

the bushes) But I heard a voice here; I should be glad to know from whence it came.

TONY: (*reassuringly*) It was I, sir, talking to myself, sir. I was saying that forty miles in four hours was very good going. *Hem.* As to be sure it was. *Hem.* I have got a sort of cold by being out in the air. We'll go in, if you please. *Hem.*

HARDCASTLE: (*puzzling*) But if you talked to yourself, you did not answer yourself. I am certain I heard two voices, and am resolved (*raising his voice*) to find the other out.

MRS. HARDCASTLE: (*gasping, from the bushes*) Oh! he's coming to find me out. Oh!

TONY: (*insistently*) What need you go, sir, if I tell you? *Hem.* I'll lay down my life for the truth—*hem*— I'll tell you all, sir. (*holding his arm to detain him*)

HARDCASTLE: (*attempting to shake himself loose*) I tell you, I will not be detained. I insist on seeing. It's in vain to expect I'll believe you.

MRS. HARDCASTLE: (*running out from behind the bushes*) O lud! he'll murder my poor boy, my darling. (*holding out her hands to Hardcastle in supplication*) Here, good gentleman, whet your rage upon me. Take my money, my life, but spare that young gentleman, spare my child, if you have any mercy.

HARDCASTLE: (*thunderstruck*) My wife, as I'm a Christian. From whence can she come, or what does she mean?

MRS. HARDCASTLE: (*moaning and kneeling*) Take compassion on us, good Mr. Highwayman. Take our money, our watches, all we have, but spare our lives. We will never bring you to justice; indeed we won't, good Mr. Highwayman.

HARDCASTLE: (*horrified*) I believe the woman's out of her senses. (*sharply, to her*) What, Dorothy, don't you know *me?*

MRS. HARDCASTLE: (*collapsing to a sitting position, overcome with relief*) Mr. Hardcastle, as I'm alive! My fears blinded me. But who, my dear, could have expected to meet you here, in this frightful place, so far from home? What has brought you to follow us?

HARDCASTLE: (*helping her to her feet*) Sure, Dorothy, you have not lost your wits? So far from home, when you are within forty yards of your own door. (*angrily, to Tony*) This is one of your old tricks, you graceless rogue you. (*with kindness, to her*) Don't you know the gate, and the mulberry tree; and don't you remember the horse-pond, my dear?

MRS. HARDCASTLE: (*vehemently*) Yes, I shall remember the horsepond as long as I live; I have caught my death in it. (*to Tony, storming*) And it is to you, you graceless varlet, I owe all this? (*raising her hand as if to strike him*) I'll teach you to abuse your mother, I will.

TONY: (*ducking*) Ecod, mother, all the parish says you have spoiled me, and so you may take the fruits on't. (*romps boisterously away toward the right*)

MRS. HARDCASTLE: (*following him with upraised hand*) I'll spoil you, I will. (*She pursues him vigorously offstage.*)

HARDCASTLE: (*as he follows slowly after them*) There's morality, however, in his reply.

He has scarcely left the stage when Hastings and Miss Neville enter from the right.

HASTINGS: (*beseechingly*) My dear Constance, why will you deliberate thus? If we delay a moment, all is lost forever. Pluck up a little resolution, and we shall soon be out of reach of her malignity.

MISS NEVILLE: (*faintly*) I find it impossible. My spirits are so sunk with the agitations I have suffered, that I am unable to face any new danger. Two or three years' patience will at last crown us with happiness.

HASTINGS: (*ardently*) Such a tedious delay is worse than inconstancy. Let us fly, my charmer. Let us date our happiness from this very moment. Perish fortune. Love and content will increase what we possess beyond a monarch's revenue. Let me prevail.

MISS NEVILLE: (*gently but firmly—sense triumphing over sensibility*) No, Mr. Hastings; no. Prudence once more comes to my relief, and I will obey its dictates. In the moment of passion, fortune may be despised, but it ever produces a lasting repentance. I'm resolved to apply to Mr. Hardcastle's compassion and justice for redress.

HASTINGS: (*dubiously*) But though he had the will, he has not the power to relieve you.

MISS NEVILLE: (*obstinately*) But he has influence, and upon that I am resolved to rely.

HASTINGS: (*moodily*) I have no hopes. But since you persist, I must reluctantly obey you.

They follow the others offstage, returning to the house.

Scene Three

The same room in the house. Sir Charles Marlow and Miss Hardcastle enter from the left at the tail end of a serious conversation.

SIR CHARLES: (*unhappily*) What a situation am I in! If what you say appears, I shall then find a guilty son. If what he says be true, I shall then lose one that, of all others, I most wished for a daughter.

MISS HARDCASTLE: (*appreciatively*) I am proud of your approbation, and to show I merit it, if you place yourselves as I directed, you shall hear his explicit declaration. (*glancing to the right*) But he comes.

SIR CHARLES: (*hurriedly*) I'll to your father, and keep him to the appointment. (*He exits rapidly to the left.*)

MARLOW: (*pensively walking on from the right*) Though prepared for setting out, I come once more to take leave, nor did I, till this moment, know the pain I feel in the separation.

MISS HARDCASTLE: (*in her own natural manner and voice*) I believe these sufferings cannot be very great, sir, which you can so easily remove. A day or two longer, perhaps, might lessen your uneasiness, by showing the little value of what you now think proper to regret.

MARLOW: (*in a surprised aside*) This girl every moment improves upon me. (*To her, with carefully controlled formality*) It must not be, madam. I have already trifled too long with my heart. My very pride begins to submit to my passion. The disparity of education and fortune, the anger of a parent, and the contempt of my equals, begin to lose their weight; and nothing can restore me to myself but this painful effort of resolution.

MISS HARDCASTLE: (*gently and in a mood of slightly theatrical pathos*) Then go, sir. I'll urge nothing more to detain you. Though my family be as good as hers you came down to visit, and my education, I hope, not inferior, what are these advantages without equal affluence? (*sighing*) I must remain contented with the slight approbation of imputed merit; I must have only the mockery of your addresses, while all your serious aims are fixed on fortune.

During this interview, Miss Hardcastle has manoeuvred him deftly into a position with his back to the screen at the left. Hardcastle and Sir Charles steal quietly through the door at the left and edge toward the screen.

SIR CHARLES: (*in a stage whisper*) Here, behind this screen.

HARDCASTLE: (*replying in kind as they vanish behind the screen, still visible to the audience but hidden from the lovers*) Ay, ay, make no noise. I'll engage my Kate covers him with confusion at last.

MARLOW: (*unable to restrain his ardor any longer*) By heavens, madam, fortune was ever my smallest consideration. Your beauty at first caught my eye; for who could see that without emotion? But every moment that I converse with you, steals in some new grace, heightens the picture, and gives it stronger expression. What at first seemed rustic plainness, now appears refined simplicity.

What seemed forward assurance, new strikes me as the result of courageous innocence and conscious virtue.

SIR CHARLES: (*in a hoarse whisper*) What can it mean? He amazes me!

HARDCASTLE: (*gleefully*) I told you how it would be. Hush!

MARLOW: (*resolutely*) I am now determined to stay, madam, and I have too good an opinion of my father's discernment, when he sees you, to doubt his approbation.

MISS HARDCASTLE: (*dramatically*) No, Mr. Marlow, I will not, cannot detain you. Do you think I could suffer a connection in which there is the smallest room for repentance? D you think I would take the mean advantage of a transient passion, to load you with confusion? Do you think I could ever relish that happiness which was acquired by lessening yours?

MARLOW: (*fervently pursuing the lure*) By all that's good, I can have no happiness but what's in *your* power to grant me! Nor shall I ever feel repentance but in not having seen your merits before. I *will* stay, even contrary to your wishes; and though you should persist to shun me, I shall make my respectful assiduities atone for the levity of my past conduct.

MISS HARDCASTLE: (*hiding her delight with difficulty while affecting a sigh of resignation*) Sir, I must entreat you'll desist. As our acquaintance began, so let it end, in indifference. I might have given an hour or two to levity; but seriously, Mr. Marlow, do you think I could ever submit to a connection where *I* must appear mercenary, and *you* imprudent? Do you think I could ever catch at the confident addresses of a secure admirer?

MARLOW: (*kneeling*) Does this look like security? Does this look like confidence? (*passionately*) No, madam, every moment that shows me your merit only serves to increase my diffidence and confusion. Here let me continue—

SIR CHARLES: (*bursting out of hiding*) I can hold it no

longer. Charles, Charles, how hast thou deceived me! Is this your indifference, your uninteresting conversation?

HARDCASTLE: (*following him out and chiming in*) Your cold contempt! your formal interview! What have you to say *now?*

MARLOW: (*overwhelmed*) That I'm all amazement! What can it mean?

HARDCASTLE: (*disdainfully*) It means that you can say and unsay things at pleasure. That you can address a lady in private, and deny it in public; that you have one story for us, and another for my daughter.

MARLOW: (*gulping*) Daughter!—this lady your daughter?

HARDCASTLE: (*as if laboring the obvious*) Yes, sir, my only daughter—my Kate; whose else should she be?

MARLOW: (*faintly*) Oh, the devil!

MISS HARDCASTLE: (*taking every advantage of the situation and teasing him outrageously*) Yes, sir, that very identical tall, squinting lady you were pleased to take me for (*curtsying*); she that you addressed as the mild, modest, sentimental man of gravity, and the bold, forward, agreeable Rattle of the Ladies' Club. Ha! ha! ha!

MARLOW: (*wishing he could sink through the floor*) Zounds, there's no bearing this; it's worse than death!

MISS HARDCASTLE: (*mercilessly*) In which of your characters, sir, will you give us leave to address you? As the faltering gentleman with looks on the ground, that speaks just to be heard, and hates hypocrisy; or the loud, confident creature, that keeps it up with Mrs. Mantrap, and old Miss Biddy Buckskin, till three in the morning? Ha! ha! ha!

MARLOW: (*in abject misery*) O, curse my noisy head! I never attempted to be impudent yet, that I was not taken down. (*like a trapped animal, looking toward the door as if it were the way out of the cage*) I must be gone.

HARDCASTLE: (*detaining him, heartily*) By the hand of my body, but you shall not. I see it was all a mistake, and I am rejoiced to find it. You shall not, sir, I tell you. I know she'll forgive you. (*to his daughter, his eyes twinkling*) Won't you forgive him, Kate? (*Her lips form a moue. He returns encouragingly to Marlow*) We'll *all* forgive you, Take courage, man.

They retire to the back scene where their conversation becomes inaudible, it being obvious only that she continues to torment him. Mrs. Hardcastle and Tony enter from the left.

MRS. HARDCASTLE: (*to Tony*) So, so, they're gone off. Let them go, I care not.

HARDCASTLE: (*speaking up and coming forward*) Who gone?

MRS. HARDCASTLE: (*with bitter sarcasm*) My dutiful niece and her gentleman, Mr. Hastings, from town. He who came down with our modest visitor here.

SIR CHARLES: (*looking up suddenly and coming forward*) Who, my honest George Hastings? As worthy a fellow who lives, and the girl could not have made a more prudent choice.

HARDCASTLE: (*beaming with pleasure*) Then, by the hand of my body, I'm proud of the connection.

MRS. HARDCASTLE: (*sourly*) Well, if he has taken away the lady, he has not taken her fortune; that remains in the family to console us for her loss.

HARDCASTLE: (*placatingly*) Sure, Dorothy, you would not be so mercenary?

MRS. HARDCASTLE: (*with acerbity*) Ay, that's my affair, not yours.

HARDCASTLE: (*pointedly*) But you know if your son, when of age, refuses to marry his cousin, her whole fortune is then at her own disposal.

MRS. HARDCASTLE: (*sharply*) Ay, but he's not of age, and she has not thought proper to wait for his refusal.

Hastings and Miss Neville appear unexpectedly in the right hand door.

MRS. HARDCASTLE: (*aside, catching sight of them*) What, returned so soon? I begin not to like it.

HASTINGS: (*approaching Hardcastle, followed by Miss Neville*) For my late attempt to fly off with your niece, let my present confusion be my punishment. We are now come back, to appeal from your justice to your humanity. By her father's consent I first paid her my addresses, and our passions were first founded in duty.

MISS NEVILLE: (*with unreserved candor*) Since his death, I have been obliged to stoop to dissimulation to avoid oppression. In an hour of levity, I was ready even to give up my fortune to secure my choice. But I am now recovered from the delusion, and hope from your tenderness what is denied me from a nearer connection. (*glancing meaningfully at her aunt*)

MRS. HARDCASTLE: (*in huffy protest*) Pshaw! pshaw, this is all but the whining end of a modern novel.

HARDCASTLE: (*affectionately*) Be it what it will, I'm glad they're come back to reclaim their due. Come hither, Tony, boy. Do you refuse this lady's hand whom I now offer you?

TONY: (*a little indignant*) What signifies my refusing? You know I can't refuse her till I'm of age, father.

HARDCASTLE: (*sombrely*) While I thought concealing your age, boy, was likely to conduce to your improvement, I concurred with your mother's desire to keep it secret. But since I find she turns it to a wrong use, I must now declare you have been of age this three months.

TONY: (*barely able to digest this revelation*) Of age! Am I of age, father?

HARDCASTLE: (*with assurance*) Above three months.

TONY: (*ecstatically*) Then you'll see the first use I'll make of my liberty. (*taking Miss Neville's hand*) Witness all men by these presents, that I, Anthony Lumpkin, Esquire, of BLANK place, refuse you, Constantia Neville, spinster, of no place at all, for my true and lawful wife. (*releasing her hand*) So Constance Neville may marry whom she pleases, (*jubilantly*) and Tony Lumpkin is his own man again.

SIR CHARLES: (*with hearty approbation*) O brave Squire!

HASTINGS: (*gratefully*) My worthy friend.

MRS. HARDCASTLE: (*sourly*) My undutiful offspring.

MARLOW: (*warmly, to Hastings as he and Miss Hardcastle come forward*) Joy, my dear George, I give you joy sincerely. (*glancing quizzically at Miss Hardcastle*) And could I prevail upon my little tyrant here to be less arbitrary, I should be the happiest man alive, if you would return me the favor.

HASTINGS: (*persuasively, to Miss Hardcastle*) Come, madam, you are now driven to the very last scene of all your contrivances. I know you like him. I'm sure he loves you, (*domineeringly*) and you *must* and *shall* have him. (*With a suspicion of a smile she blushes and lowers her head in happy submission.*)

HARDCASTLE: (*joining their hands as she raises her head and looks fondly at Marlow*) And I say so, too. And, Mr. Marlow, if she makes as good a wife as she has a daughter, I don't believe you'll ever repent your bargain. (*addressing the entire group*) So now to supper. Tomorrow we shall gather all the poor of the parish about us, and the MISTAKES OF THE NIGHT shall be crowned with a merry morning. (*with robust affection, to Marlow*) So, boy, take her; and as you have been mistaken in the mistress, my wish is, that you may never be mistaken in the wife.

EPILOGUE

(spoken by Mrs. Bulkley in the character of Miss Hardcastle)

Well, having stooped to conquer with success,
And gained a husband without aid from dress,
Still, as a barmaid, I could wish it too,
As I have conquered him to conquer you:
And let me say, for all your resolution,
That pretty barmaids have done execution.
Our life is all a play, composed to please;
"We have our exits and our entrances."[1]
The first act shows the simple country maid,
Harmless and young, of everything afraid;
Blushes when hired, and with unmeaning action,
"I hopes as how to give you satisfaction."
Her second act displays a livelier scene,—
Th'unblushing barmaid of a country inn,
Who whisks about the house, at market caters,
Talks loud, coquettes the guests, and scolds the waiters.
Next the scene shifts to town, and there she soars,
The chophouse toast of ogling connoisseurs.
On squires and cits[2] she there displays her arts,
And on the gridiron broils her lovers' hearts;
And as she smiles, her triumphs to complete,
Even common councilmen forget to eat.
The fourth act shows her wedded to the Squire,
And Madam now begins to hold it higher;
Pretends to taste, at Operas cries *caro*,[3]

---

1 Shakespeare, *As You Like It,* Act II, Scene 7.
2 Citizens, or common people.
3 Literally "beloved," a traditional cry of approval like *bravo.*

And quits her "Nancy Dawson" for "Che Faro":[4]
Dotes upon dancing, and in all her pride,
Swims round the room, the Heinel of Cheapside;[5]
Ogles and leers, with artificial skill,
Till, having lost in age the power to kill,
She sits all night at cards, and ogles at spadille.[6]
Such, through our lives, the eventful history—
The fifth and last act still remains for me:
The barmaid now for your protection prays,
Turns female barrister, and pleads for Bayes.[7]

EPILOGUE

by Joseph Cradock, Esq.

*intended to be spoken in the character of Tony Lumpkin,
written by a friend of Goldsmith's after reading the manuscript of the play. This abridged version accompanied
the printed edition.*

Well, now all's ended, and my comrades gone,
Pray what becomes of *mother's nonly son?*
A hopeful blade!—in town I'll fix my station,
And try to make a bluster in the nation.
As for my cousin Neville, I renounce her,
Off, in a crack, I'll carry big Bet Bouncer.
Why should not I in the great world appear?
I soon shall have a thousand pounds a year;
No matter what a man may here inherit,

---

[4] Gives up popular songs like "Nancy Dawson" for operatic
arias like the "Che Faro" in Gluck's *Orfeo*.

[5] That is, she would appeal to the low taste of vulgar Cheapside
and be as sensational as the French danseuse Anna Heinel was
with those of cultivated taste.

[6] The ace of spades.

[7] Goldsmith is referring to himself as an amateur playwright
by adopting the name of *Bayes,* a character of that type in Buck-
ingham's *The Rehearsal* (1671).

In London—gad, they've some regard to spirit.
I see the horses prancing up the streets,
And big Bet Bouncer bobs to all she meets;
Then hoiks to jigs and pastimes every night—
Not to the plays—they say it an't polite:
To Sadler's Wells,[1] perhaps, or operas go,
And once by chance, to the roratorio.[2]
Thus here and there, forever up and down,
We'll set the fashions too, to half the town;
And then at auctions—money ne'er regard,
Buy pictures, like the great, ten pounds a yard;
Zounds, we shall make these London gentry say,
We know what's damned genteel, as well as they!

---

[1] An amusement resort on the outskirts of London.
[2] Tony's version of *oratorio*.

BIBLIOGRAPHY

THE PLAYWRIGHT

Austin Dobson, *Life of Oliver Goldsmith*. London: W. Scott, 1888.

William Freeman, *Oliver Goldsmith*. London: Herbert Jenkins, 1951.

Stephen Gwynn, *Oliver Goldsmith*. London: T. Butterworth, 1935.

Ralph M. Wardle, *Oliver Goldsmith*. Kansas City: University of Kansas Press, 1958.

THE PLAY

She Stoops to Conquer, edited by John Hampden. New York: E. P. Dutton & Co., 1927.

She Stoops to Conquer, notes by Robert Herring. London: St. Martins, 1935.

The Plays of Oliver Goldsmith, edited by C. E. Doble. London: Oxford University Press, 1909, 1936.

THE STAGING

Allardyce Nicoll, *The Development of the Theatre*. London: G. G. Harrop & Co., 1937.

Richard Southern, *Changeable Scenery, Its Origin and Development in the English Theatre*. London: Faber and Faber, 1951.